Books by Dennis M Keating

The Olympics:
An Unauthorized Unsanctioned History
*

Charlie Whitman
Was a Friend of Mine
*

Ena Road
*

The Fulda Gap
*

A Chicago Tale
*

Black Lahu
*

Poetry for Men

Poetry for Men

Action Adventure
Murder

Dennis M Keating

This book was created by
Dennis M Keating, the Honolulu Guy,
in coordination with the Golden Sphere team.

The Author

Dennis M Keating

is
The Honolulu Guy

DEDICATION

To my three children,
Patrick, Maureen & Tara,
who, just maybe,
don't know everything
their father has done.

ACKNOWLEDMENTS

Thanks to

Professor Steven Taylor Goldsberry
My Mentor

Paula Marie Fernandez
and Hikari Kimura
For Artwork & Maps

Gail M Baugniet and
Faith Scheideman
Advisors & Proofreaders

Joei Gomez
Assistance & Technical Support

Sandy
My Wife, Proponent & Ally

Poetry for Men

Action Adventure Murder

Five Narrative Poems
written in
Rhyming Couplets
BY
DENNIS M KEATING

This book is a compilation
of the author's first five poetry books:

Charlie Whitman Was a Friend of Mine
Ena Road
The Fulda Gap
A Chicago Tale
Black Lahu

Dennis M Keating, the author of **Poetry for Men,** has enjoyed a rather peripatetic life. His stories reflect this as each takes place in a different locale – Germany, Thailand, Hawaii, Texas and Chicago.

All five stories are true. Four relate to Keating's personal experiences. The fifth took place almost ninety years ago, but its initial incident occurred just a half block from Keating's current home.

The stories are written for male audiences as they include action, adventure and/or murder in their central themes. While these tales have gritty elements, many women will also appreciate them.

Each story is written in a poetic, rhyming couplet format. Hopefully, this approach will encourage more men to develop an interest in verse and expand the realm of poetry. Trustfully, all audiences, male and female, will find the five tales interesting and compelling.

Poetry for Men

Action Adventure Murder

Page

Charlie Whitman
Was a Friend of Mine

The Texas Tower
Killer Marine

DEDICATION

This poem is dedicated to all the victims of the Texas Tower Massacre and their families. We honor and recognize the seventeen innocent individuals who were murdered in cold blood by Charlie Whitman. We also honor the many individuals who were shot and injured, and the countless others who suffered heartbreak because they lost family members and friends.

On August 1, 1966, Charles Whitman was gunned down on the observation deck of the University of Texas Tower in Austin, Texas. In the fourteen hours prior to this, Whitman had shot, knifed and bludgeoned to death seventeen people and injured many more.

Whitman was a former US Marine. Two years prior to the rampage, Whitman served in the Marine Corps at Camp Lejeune, North Carolina.

One of Whitman's fellow Marines at Lejeune was Dennis M. Keating, the author of this story. Whitman and Keating were friends. As a matter of fact, Whitman was the battalion duty clerk, the night Keating was discharged from the Corps. That night, Whitman personally handed Keating his discharge papers. Whitman was the last Marine to whom Keating said goodbye. The two friends never met again.

Keating had been the battalion payroll clerk. Keating got to know Whitman because of this. When Whitman was court martialed, he was demoted. He lost his rank, and lost a large chunk of his pay. As Keating handled Whitman's payroll records, he had to advise Whitman during this critical period. Due to his position, Keating had access to and read Whitman's court martial papers.

Keating still carries the strong impression he had of Whitman from the very first day they met. Keating remembers thinking back then, if he were ever to make a Hollywood feature film about the Marine Corps, he would ask the polite, handsome, and squared away Whitman to play the lead role. At the time, Keating considered Whitman to be a true Marine's Marine.

Now, fifty years later, for the first time, Keating tells his personal story about his old friend and fellow Marine, Charlie Whitman, **The Texas Tower Killer.**

Backstory

One evening in early October 1964, just before midnight, I entered the office of the Headquarters Battalion of the 2nd Marine Division at Camp Lejeune, North Carolina, to pick up my discharge papers. The clerk on duty was my friend, Charles Whitman. I signed the papers. We chatted briefly, shook hands and said goodbye. Two hours later I was on an early morning bus to Washington, D.C.

I pretty much forgot about Charlie and my other Marine Corps buddies until twenty-two months later.

On August 1st, 1966. I left my office at the Chicago Police headquarters to catch a subway train home. I bought the evening newspaper; saw Charlie's picture on the front page and read the headline story.

I first met Charlie
through my Marine Corps work.

My MOS,
2nd Marine Division, Payroll Clerk.

I handled the Headquarters Battalion
payroll stuff,

And kept the money
and numbers up to snuff.

I'd just returned from
a Chitown Thanksgiving holiday.

Now, back at Lejeune,
I was computing leatherneck pay.

MOS – Marine Corps term for **Military Occupational Specialty.**

Chitown – A nickname for Chicago

Lejeune – Camp Lejeune, North Carolina, the main Marine Corps base on the east coast of the USA. Lejeune is the home of the 2nd Marine Division.

Leatherneck – A nickname for a Marine

The (Three) Musketeers - Romantic and brave heroes from French literature.

Larry, Moe and Curley - the first names of The Three Stooges, a slapstick comedy trio, popular in the movies and television during the mid-twentieth century.

JFK – **President John F. Kennedy** was assassinated in Dallas on November 22, 1963. His killer was **Lee Harvey Oswald**. Two days later, Oswald was murdered by Jack Ruby, the owner of a sleazy Dallas strip joint.

Who can forget
November '63?

Dallas, Oswald
and Kennedy.

Texas. Marines. Guns.
They're birds of a feather.

Too often, it seems,
they fly together.

Maybe, like the musketeers,
they're an intertwined three.

Ultra-Liberals might say:
more like Larry, Moe, and Curley.

Texas
School Book
Depository
Dallas, Texas

November 22, 1963

Those were not happy times
in the USA.
JFK's death had put a chill
on Thanksgiving Day.

At home in Chicago,
my folks remained sad.

So, being back at Lejeune
kinda made me feel glad.

Shortly after, I met Charlie;
He'd been busted to E-1.

His pay was cut.
Certainly not fun.

Lee Harvey Oswald

Conspiracy theorists claim Oswald was a patsy controlled by others and not a lone assassin. No. Oswald was a stupid, screw up. He was too unreliable to trust.

As a troubled teen, Oswald said **Life Sucks** and joined the Marines. After a troubling time in the Corps, Oswald said **The Marines Suck**, I want to go home and help my Mom. The Marines gave Oswald a **Compassionate Discharge**. Within a few days of arriving home, Oswald said **the USA Sucks, I wanna be a communist and live in Russia**. Oswald moved to Moscow to live his communist dream. In Russia, he publically denounced the USA and told the US Embassy he planned to renounce his US citizenship. TASS, the soviet news agency, loved it; the Marines not so much. As Oswald was still in the Marine Reserves, they said, **You don't wanna be an American? You Suck.** They gave Oswald an **Undesirable Discharge**.

The Ruskies got 15 minutes of PR news from Oswald. They soon realized **Oswald sucked** and was an unstable nut case. They sent him to work in an out of town, factory assembly line. Oswald was crushed. His dream of being an international political Rock Star were shattered. Deeply depressed he attempted suicide. As with other things, he failed. He then returned to the US Embassy singing: ***This place Sucks. Please let me go home.***

Back in Texas, no one wanted to hire a rude, arrogant, **Undesirable** Marine. Also, Oswald was obnoxious. Most people disliked him. Previously, he had written to fellow Fort Worther and former **Navy Secretary, John Connally,** begging his discharge be changed to **Honorable**. Oswald didn't get a response. Connally became Governor of Texas. Oswald became furious. ***You made my life Suck.*** He sought total, bloody revenge at Connally and the military. In April 1963, Oswald tried to shoot former General Edwin Walker through his dining room window. An easy shot. Oswald missed.

Oswald was *Osvaldovich* to his fellow Marines. A dysfunctional **Shitbird.** A lousy Marine, and a lousy shot. Many Marines believed Oswald was the lone shooter and Governor Connally was his real target. To us, Oswald was a screwed-up dude. He pulled the trigger and missed Connally and caused Kennedy to become unintended collateral damage.

Prior to this, Oswald had opened a post office box for his mail order weapons and ammo. For this, Oswald, a voracious reader, created a pseudonym, *Alek J. Hidell.* This was Oswald's adjusted anagram for *Jekyll/Hyde*, the duel personality, good/evil character created by the author, Robert Lewis Stevenson. Oswald had a kinship with the frustrated and psychologically troubled Dr. Jekyll. For the dysfunctional Oswald, his inexact anagram was clever. *I'm a genius. The world sucks for not seeing my greatness.*

Most grunts who got busted
were screwed-up dudes,

Full of anger at the Corps
and hateful attitudes.

We called 'em Shitbirds,
Pitiful, short-circuited dopes.

They'd lost their self-respect;
Along with their hopes.

These demoted losers yelled at me,
As I tried my best.

They were hurting bad inside,
And now they were paid less.

Jarhead – Nickname for a Marine

E-1 – A private. The lowest rank, in the Marines.

Grunt – Nickname for a Marine.

Shitbird – A nickname for a screwed up, f*cked up Marine.

Squared Away – A well-organized, neat and disciplined Marine. As well as being combat efficient, 24-7, all Marines are also required to be squared away at all times. Often, those Marines who were reduced in rank to the lowest level, E-1, simply gave up and no longer cared. They knew it is just a matter of time, before they were kicked out of the Marine Corps for good.

I anticipated
An angry jarhead facing me.

This was not true for Charlie.
He was polite as he could be.

His uniform was neatly pressed
And spotlessly clean.

Nodding with respect,
Here stood a Squared Away Marine.

We worked out his payroll math
For an hour that day.

His wife's benefits were cut sharply
Due to his decreased pay.

Court Martial - A military trial that determines if a Marine is guilty of a crime. If so, a punishment is then determined. A court marital does not mean expulsion from the military. In Charlie's case, he was demoted in rank and served a certain punishment time. He then was brought in once again as a full Marine.

The Uniform Code of Military Justice allows for lesser forms of punishment than a court martial for minor violations of military law. During his tour of duty, the author often saw higher-ups look the other way, or mete out much lesser punishments for the same infractions that Charlie Whitman was found guilty.

Been had – Cheated or falsely set up. Charlie's situation is comparable to the scene in the film *Casablanca*, when Captain Renault is shocked to find gambling in Rick's Casino.

That next month, Charlie came back
More than twice.

He showed no visible anger.
He was always polite and nice.

In Charlie's files, his court martial
Papers caught my eye.

I read them one night
After bidding him goodbye.

What I read baffled me.
I felt Charlie had been had.

His three so-called crimes
Were simply nothing bad.

SOP - Standard Operating Procedure. In slang usage, SOP means something that is very common or always happens.

Russian Roulette - A dangerous game played with a loaded pistol. The shooter holds a revolver to his side after placing a single bullet in one of the cylinder's six chambers. The cylinder is spun; the pistol is raised to the head and the trigger is pulled.

In our Marine Corps unit, the guys played several modified and safer versions of Russian Roulette. In one version, the shooter held his arm down at his side, so he could quickly glance to see if a bullet was in a visible chamber. If he took too much time looking, he was labeled a **Chicken** or a coward. His speed at bringing the pistol up to his head and pulling the trigger was viewed as a gauge of his manliness and bravery.

I pondered the words I read,

And couldn't figure them out.

After all, this is the Marine Corps
We're talking about.

Busted for gambling. What?
Are you kidding me?

In the Corps,
Friday night poker games were S.O.P.

Busted for an extra weapon.
A hip pocket gun.

Give me a break.
Half the enlisted packed one.

In our second version of Russian Roulette, the shooter pointed a revolver at a target person. The target person said to fire or not fire. Then, the shooter pulled the trigger. If the target said not to fire and there was no bullet in the chamber, the target person was labeled a **Chicken**. Nineteen-year-old Marines do not like to be called **Chicken**.

The author knew of several incidents of guys getting wounded and was present at one incident that was covered up.

15 for 20 – Giving a loan of $15.00 and collecting $20.00 a few days later. During the 1960's, the Marines lined up and were paid in cash. The payroll clerk would get back his loan and interest immediately when the Marine was handed his money. Often, payroll clerks were paid on Fridays and the rest of the Marines on Monday. This allowed payroll clerks to give out weekend loans and make interest money from the loans.

In our payroll office,
On any weekend day,

Our version of Russian Roulette
Was the in game to play.

Who was a chicken?
Who was not?

Naturally, sometimes,
A guy got shot.

We'd just patch up the wounds
And hide all the facts,

And keep the details hidden
From the higher-ups' backs.

C.O. – The Commanding Officer of a Marine company. Normally, a company C.O is a Captain who commands up to 200 members.

Louie – Or Luey or Lewey – A slang term for either a Second Lieutenant or a First Lieutenant ranks Officers start as Second Lieutenants. After satisfactory time and performance, they are promoted to First Lieutenants. Later, they are promoted to Captain. These are Company Level Ranks.

Battalions usually consist of five or six companies and have field grade officers: Majors, Lieutenant Colonels and Colonels.

Battalion officers conduct court martials. The author believes a company level officer must have convinced a battalion officer that Charlie's minor infractions warranted a court marital trial, rather than the more normal, lesser judicial procedure. The author's attempts to uncover the backstory were unsuccessful.

Busted for lending money
With interest! That's a crime?

We payroll clerks
Did it all the time.

We'd pay ourselves early
Before the weekend;

Then offer 15 for 20,
To grunts eager to spend.

To me, this court martial thing
really stank.

Some officer had it in for Charlie,
One who had a bit of rank.

Sign at the entrance of Camp Lejeune, North Carolina.

I figured his C.O. pushed it,
While trying to guess who.

A 2nd or 1st Louie couldn't
shove this garbage through.

Due to Charlie's payroll issues,
He became a casual friend.

I really liked the guy
And hoped he'd mend.

If we met on the street,
I'd always stop and chat.

At least a "How's it going?"
And other stuff like that.

He'd earned back a Stripe - He'd been promoted back to a former rank. In Charlie's case, he had started, as all enlisted Marines do, as a Private (E-1). During his career, he had risen to Lance Corporal (E-3). His court martial trial reduced him back to the basic enlisted rank of (E-1), a rank that has no stripes on its uniform's arm. At the time of our last meeting, Charlie had started to move back up again and had recently become a Private First Class (E-2).

Life moved forward
Until October '64.

My time was up.
I was done with the Corps.

With bags packed heavy
and my spirits light,

I was happy to see
Charlie on duty that night.

He'd earned back a Stripe.
He was turning out to be real.

Good goin', Charlie Boy.
We both know you got a raw deal.

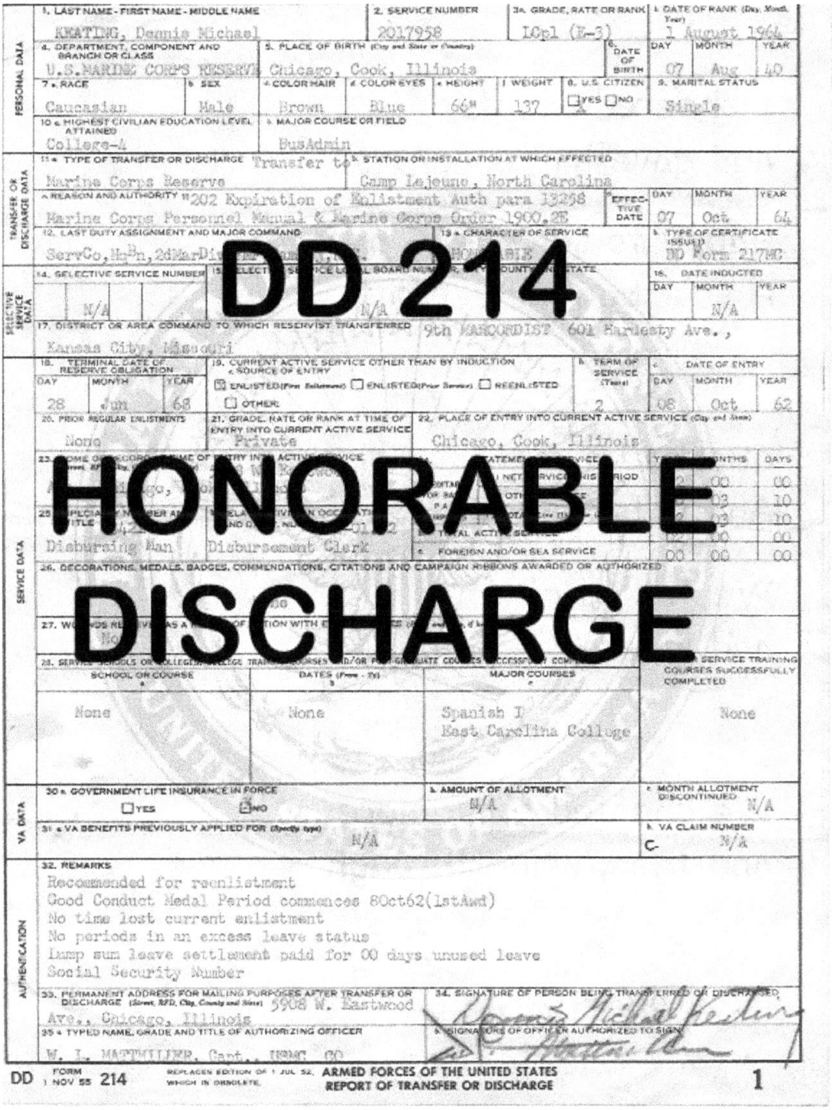

DD 214
HONORABLE
DISCHARGE

PERSONAL DATA
1. LAST NAME - FIRST NAME - MIDDLE NAME: KEATING, Dennis Michael
2. SERVICE NUMBER: 2017958
3a. GRADE, RATE OR RANK: LCpl (E-3)
b. DATE OF RANK (Day, Month, Year): 1 August 1964
4. DEPARTMENT, COMPONENT AND BRANCH OR CLASS: U.S.MARINE CORPS RESERVE
5. PLACE OF BIRTH (City and State or Country): Chicago, Cook, Illinois
6. DATE OF BIRTH: DAY 07 MONTH Aug YEAR 40
7a. RACE: Caucasian
b. SEX: Male
c. COLOR HAIR: Brown
d. COLOR EYES: Blue
e. HEIGHT: 66"
f. WEIGHT: 137
8. U.S. CITIZEN: ☐ YES ☐ NO
9. MARITAL STATUS: Single
10a. HIGHEST CIVILIAN EDUCATION LEVEL ATTAINED: College-4
b. MAJOR COURSE OR FIELD: BusAdmin

TRANSFER OR DISCHARGE DATA
11a. TYPE OF TRANSFER OR DISCHARGE: Transfer to Marine Corps Reserve
b. STATION OR INSTALLATION AT WHICH EFFECTED: Camp Lejeune, North Carolina
c. REASON AND AUTHORITY: #202 Expiration of Enlistment Auth para 13258 Marine Corps Personnel Manual & Marine Corps Order 1900.2E
d. EFFECTIVE DATE: DAY 07 MONTH Oct YEAR 64
12. LAST DUTY ASSIGNMENT AND MAJOR COMMAND: ServCo,HqBn,2dMarDiv
13a. CHARACTER OF SERVICE: HONORABLE
b. TYPE OF CERTIFICATE ISSUED: DD Form 217MC

SELECTIVE SERVICE DATA
14. SELECTIVE SERVICE NUMBER: N/A
15. SELECTIVE SERVICE LOCAL BOARD NUMBER, CITY, COUNTY AND STATE: N/A
16. DATE INDUCTED: DAY MONTH YEAR N/A
17. DISTRICT OR AREA COMMAND TO WHICH RESERVIST TRANSFERRED: 9th MARCORDIST 601 Hardesty Ave., Kansas City, Missouri

SERVICE DATA
18. TERMINAL DATE OF RESERVE OBLIGATION: DAY 28 MONTH Jun YEAR 68
19. CURRENT ACTIVE SERVICE OTHER THAN BY INDUCTION
a. SOURCE OF ENTRY: ☒ ENLISTED (First Enlistment) ☐ ENLISTED (Prior Service) ☐ REENLISTED ☐ OTHER
b. TERM OF SERVICE (Years): 2
c. DATE OF ENTRY: DAY 08 MONTH Oct YEAR 62
20. PRIOR REGULAR ENLISTMENTS: None
21. GRADE, RATE OR RANK AT TIME OF ENTRY INTO CURRENT ACTIVE SERVICE: Private
22. PLACE OF ENTRY INTO CURRENT ACTIVE SERVICE (City and State): Chicago, Cook, Illinois
23. HOME OF RECORD AT TIME OF ENTRY INTO ACTIVE SERVICE
24. STATEMENT OF SERVICE: YEARS MONTHS DAYS
a. NET SERVICE THIS PERIOD: 2 00 00
b. OTHER: 03 10
c. TOTAL: 2 03 10
d. TOTAL ACTIVE SERVICE: 00 00
e. FOREIGN AND/OR SEA SERVICE: 00 00 00
25. RELATED CIVILIAN OCCUPATION AND D.O.T. NUMBER: Disbursing Man; Disbursement Clerk
26. DECORATIONS, MEDALS, BADGES, COMMENDATIONS, CITATIONS AND CAMPAIGN RIBBONS AWARDED OR AUTHORIZED
27. WOUNDS RECEIVED AS A RESULT OF ACTION WITH ENEMY FORCES
28. SERVICE SCHOOLS OR COLLEGES, COLLEGE TRAINING COURSES AND/OR POST-GRADUATE COURSES SUCCESSFULLY COMPLETED
a. SCHOOL OR COURSE: None
b. DATES (From - To): None
c. MAJOR COURSES: Spanish I, East Carolina College
29. OTHER SERVICE TRAINING COURSES SUCCESSFULLY COMPLETED: None

VA DATA
30a. GOVERNMENT LIFE INSURANCE IN FORCE: ☐ YES ☒ NO
b. AMOUNT OF ALLOTMENT: N/A
c. MONTH ALLOTMENT DISCONTINUED: N/A
31a. VA BENEFITS PREVIOUSLY APPLIED FOR (Specify type): N/A
b. VA CLAIM NUMBER: C- N/A

AUTHENTICATION
32. REMARKS
Recommended for reenlistment
Good Conduct Medal Period commences 8Oct62(1stAwd)
No time lost current enlistment
No periods in an excess leave status
Lump sum leave settlement paid for 00 days unused leave
Social Security Number
33. PERMANENT ADDRESS FOR MAILING PURPOSES AFTER TRANSFER OR DISCHARGE (Street, RFD, City, County and State): 5908 W. Eastwood Ave., Chicago, Illinois
34. SIGNATURE OF PERSON BEING TRANSFERRED OR DISCHARGED
35a. TYPED NAME, GRADE AND TITLE OF AUTHORIZING OFFICER: W. L. MATTMILLER, Capt., USMC CO
b. SIGNATURE OF OFFICER AUTHORIZED TO SIGN

DD FORM 1 NOV 55 214 REPLACES EDITION OF 1 JUL 52, WHICH IS OBSOLETE. ARMED FORCES OF THE UNITED STATES REPORT OF TRANSFER OR DISCHARGE 1

A DD 214, the standard Discharge Paper.

I cheered silently
and gave him congrats.

Happy to see a PFC bested
A scumbag officer rat.

Charlie gave me my discharge
And noted my happy glow.

We talked of what I'd do,
and where I'd go.

We chatted some more
and then, when through,

Shook hands, and Charlie said,
"God be with you!"

Congrats - Congratulations

PFC - Private First Class

Scumbag – Slang for someone who is viewed as contemptible.

I never thought I'd see
Charlie's face again.

Then, some two years later,
on a Chicago subway train,

The front-page news splash
was clear to see.

Charlie's easy-going smile
was looking straight at me.

The story noted
The hot summer day.

Austin, Texas in August?
Sure, it's always that way.

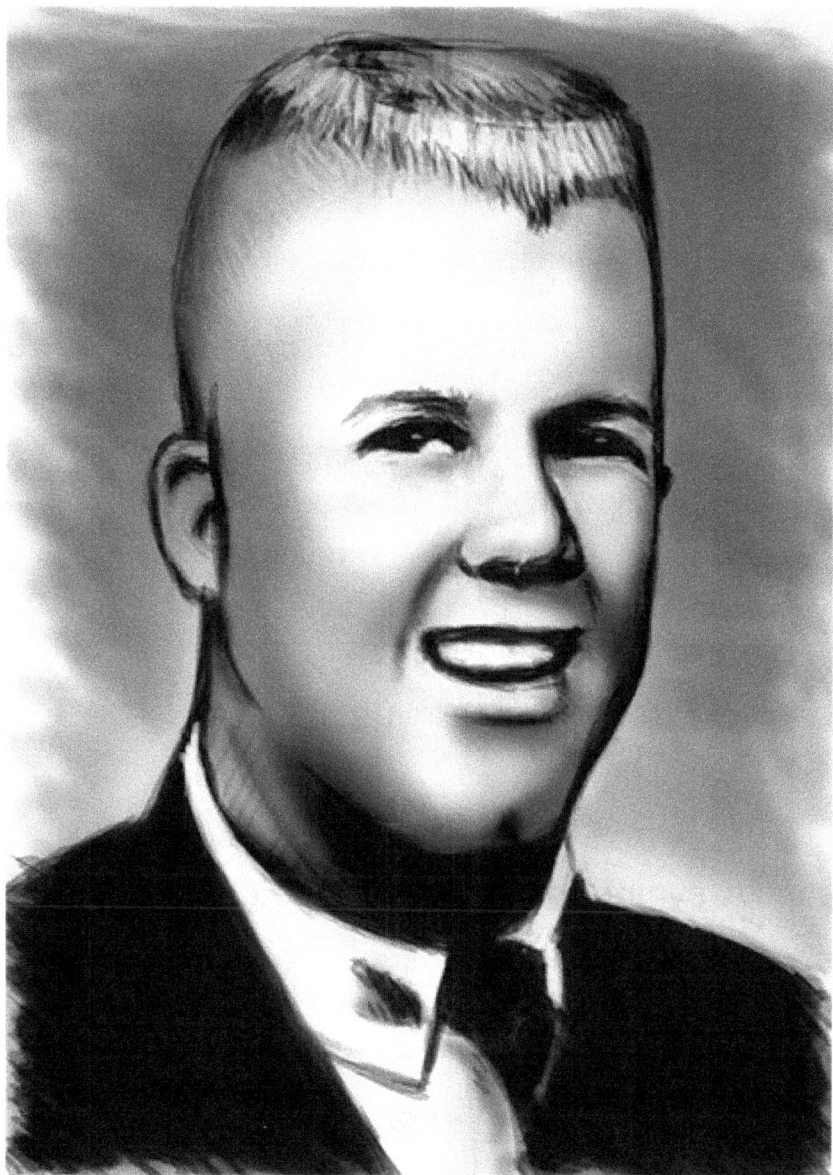

People sitting in the sun;
Children at play.

Totally unaware
They had become human prey.

The University of Texas Tower,
Three hundred feet tall.

A very imposing sight
Across the green mall.

"A symbol of Academic Excellence,"
The website now reads.

It doesn't mention bloody bodies
Or a Marine's killing deeds.

When the first shot rang out,
No one bothered to look.

They were napping,
Idly chatting, or reading a book.

The first student, a co-ed, fell.
No one looked around.

Her boyfriend asked, "What's wrong?"
As she hit the ground.

Those few words
were the last he ever said.

A few seconds later,
He was down, bloody and dead.

Next killed: a Ph.D.,
A visiting professor of math.

Picked off on the South Mall.
He didn't count on that.

A Marine sharpshooter.
A high tower and a 360° view.

Picking off marks was easy.
Like shooting hippos in a zoo.

A Remington 700 rifle
With a sniper scope.

Targets within 300 yards
Had no hope.

Emergency! Emergency!

A police switchboard operator

Fear filled people's faces.
Some uncontrollably cried.

A few more bang-bangs.
Everyone scurried to hide.

Flooded with uncertainty.
Which way to go?

What's happening?
There was no way to know.

Just minutes into it,
the police phone started to ring.

"Hurry to campus!
It's all crazy. Someone's shooting!"

That ain't Shootin'

That's

Marine Corps Shootin'

An individual ducking for cover

More calls went out.
"We need every cop in town."

"Emergency! Emergency!"
"Another body down."

Young Patrolman Speed
was the first cop to arrive.

Speed wasn't fast enough.
Bang-bang. He was no longer alive.

Then a few gutsy officers
Reached the tower base.

All held stoic looks. They knew
The danger they'd faced.

For ninety minutes, Whitman shot at and killed strangers who were walking at or near the University of Texas. After a short time, he was confronted by return fire from numerous weapons carried by various citizens of Texas who were in the area. Do you know how many Central Texas Good Ol' Boys carry weapons in their pickup truck?

Up the elevator, they peered
Cautiously out the door.

Their quick glances saw bloody bodies
sprawled on the floor.

One cop signals,
You go left; we go right.

One crossed himself. He knew
This would be a death fight.

Fortune sided with the police.
Charlie was caught by surprise.

Hardly a second to react
When he saw their eyes.

Blam!
Blam!
Blam!

A gun

A pistol rang out,
Then a shotgun.

Blam! Blam! Blam!
Charlie was done.

The total tally?
Some 17 dead,

Thirty plus transported
to a hospital bed.

During the next few hours
Things quieted down.

During the next few months,
Charlie was the talk of the town.

One Shot

One Kill

A Marine Corps Tradition

TV anchors watched
as their ratings shot high.

Just like JFK's death, there were
Theories and questions of why.

America's first mass murder
in nearly ten years.

All wrapped up by Prime Time.
Media barons gave cheers.

For corporate networks,
It was nice, clean, and tight.

Ad revenues went up by airing
A new detail every night.

Clutter Farmhouse - This refers to the nonsensical killing of the Clutter family in small town Iowa in November 1959. Initially, the crime received little national news coverage. Six years later, at the end of 1965, the author, Truman Capote, published the book, **In Cold Blood**.

In Cold Blood, presented a detailed account of the killing; the killers, and the victims. The book became a bestseller just months before the Texas Tower killings. This book made many publishers and media executives realize they could make money from the public's fascination with sensational killings.

This Texas Tower Massacre
was a real visual deal.

Not like the Clutter Farmhouse
In a remote Kansas field.

The news bosses realized
for a month or two

That any new fact or twist
meant extra revenue.

A Texas Tower pic could catch
more eyeballs on the 10 PM news

Than a bikini-clad gal
dishing out free booze.

Requiescat In Pace

A Catholic Priest

Now, 50 years have passed.
Still, many questions remain.

Perhaps more will come,
With more theories to explain.

What factors make a mass killer
Out of an average Joe?

Childhood beatings? Brain tumor?
We'll never actually know.

Now, when driving on I-35,
Down Austin way,

I say a silent prayer
For those poor souls killed that day.

Semper Fi

Semper Fi – Always Faithful. The Marine Corps greeting.

Semper Fi - The shortened form of the Latin phrase, **Semper Fidelis**, the motto of the US Marine Corps. In English, **Semper Fidelis** means **Always Faithful.**

Then, one more for my fellow Marine, As I look to the sky.

"God be with you, Charlie!"

And yes, **"Semper Fi."**

University of Texas

24th St

The Drag - Guadalupe St

Speedway

University of Texas
Main Campus

Littlefield Fountain

21st St

Murder Victims of Charlie Whitman

Family Members

Margaret Whitman – Charlie Whitman's mother. Killed in her home.

Kathy Whitman - Whitman's wife. Killed in their home.

Killed inside the Texas Tower

Edna Townsley - A Tower receptionist.

Martin Gabour - A Tower visitor.
A service station manager.

Marguerite Lamport - A Tower visitor.
A housewife.

Killed on the University campus

Baby Boy Wilson - Shot in the womb of his six-month pregnant mother, Claire Wilson, Claire survived the shooting.

Patrolman Billy Speed - The first Austin police officer to respond to the massacre.

Robert Boyer - A visiting mathematics professor.

Thomas Ashton - A Peace Corps trainee.

Thomas Eckman - A UT student.

Roy Schmidt - A city electrician.

David Gunby - A UT student. Gunby required ongoing dialysis treatment for thirty-five years. Finally, in 2001, because of the ongoing pain, Gunby chose to stop the dialysis. He died a few days later.

Killed in the Guadalupe Street area

Karen Griffith - A high school student.

Thomas Karr - A UT student.

Claudia Rutt - A recent high school graduate.

Paul Sonntag - A recent high school graduate.

Harry Walchuk - A UT graduate student.

The Aftermath

Shortly after the Texas Tower killings, Texas Governor John Connally ordered an investigation into the incident and into the perpetrator, Charles Whitman.

One month later, in September 1966, the Connally Commission issued a report entitled: ***Medical Aspects of the Charles J. Whitman Catastrophe.*** The report stated Whitman did have a **brain tumor**, but the commission could not determine with clarity the tumor's impact on Whitman's mental state.

Also noted was Whitman's hostility toward his father. This related to the **terrible domestic abuse** Whitman, his siblings and his mother suffered under his nasty and truly evil, control freak father.

The author believes both issues played major roles in the killings.

Charlie's Family

Charlie's father, C. A. Whitman, Jr. was the epitome of a physically and mentally abusive husband and father. C. A. believed he had the right to punch out and psychologically devastate his wife and children regularly for any disagreement or minor shortcoming. He always demanded excellence from his children, and, he used physical abuse if they fell short of the unrealistic goals he set for them.

Until his death, C.A. lived in total denial concerning his domestic violence crimes against his wife and children. His main pride was a collection of sixty guns that included two machine guns.

Less than 90 days after his wife was buried, C.A. remarried. His new wife, 23, had a 3-year-old son. The marriage lasted just a few weeks, with the divorce related to C.A. severely beating her son.

C.A. quickly married again for a third time to the mother of the wife of his son, John.

This marriage lasted longer than the second marriage, but was continually marred by C.A.'s violent rages.

Charlie's mother, Margaret Whitman, was the textbook example of the Battered Wife Syndrome. In May 1966, less than three months before Charlie's killing rampage, Margaret worked up the courage to leave her long abusive husband and their home in Florida. Charlie drove to Florida to bring his mother to Austin to live near him.

Charlie's youngest brother, John, at age 18, got married within a year of the Texas Tower killings. He was killed in a barroom fight in 1973 at age 24. His widow later died as a heroin addict.

Charlie's other brother, Patrick, married at age 20, a year before the Tower killings. In 1973, around the time his brother, John, was killed, Patrick announced to his wife that he was gay. He chose to move out of their home and move to California. He died of AIDS while living in Los Angeles.

.

God
be wîth
you!

Ena Road

Murder in Old Honolulu

DEDICATION

To the victims of
Racism and Prejudice
throughout our world.

Ena Road tells of the *Massie Affair*, a series of events that took place in Honolulu in 1931 and 1932.

The *Massie Affair* concerned a 20-year-old woman with serious emotional and psychological issues, who was assaulted on *Ena Road*. The young lady's jaw was broken. The lady, a Caucasian and, a US Navy Officer's wife, claimed she had also been gang raped by a group of locals. The examining doctors stated a rape did not occur. The local men she accused were of Asian and Polynesian ethnicity. The time line of events showed the locals could not have been at the scene of the crime. The trial resulted in a hung jury, but the story does not end there.

Naturally, racism, prejudice, social status and politics entered the equation. In the end, the Massie Affair had a strong impact on Hawaii and resonated across America to the halls of power in Washington D.C.

In 1931, Hawaii was very segregated. Local Asians and Polynesians did not interact socially with members of the navy or for that matter, any Caucasians.

As the navy, was totally male, virtually all the women at the **Ala Wai Club** were navy wives or family members. Among the sailors, there was sharp competition for the company of the few available females. This resulted in unmarried sailors becoming overly aggressive in their pursuit of single Caucasian women.

During the 1920's and '30's, prostitution was a thriving industry in the Hotel Street and Chinatown areas of downtown Honolulu. While the prostitutes would service both military men and local men, separate waiting rooms were maintained, as the Caucasian sailors did not want to know the woman who they were paying for had previously been with a local man.

Waikiki is approximately three miles from downtown Honolulu. In 1931, Waikiki tourism was a slow growing toddler. Also, Waikiki was small scale. Its clientele was somewhat elitist and pretty much limited to upper classes, movie stars and others with money. Things didn't really change until after World War II, when airplanes rather than ships became the more popular way to cross the Pacific.

Waikiki's first major hotel, the Moana, opened in 1901. A few hundred yards down the beach, around 1915, a group of residential bungalows evolved into the Halekulani Resort. In the mid 1920's, one of its guests, the mystery novel author, Earl Derr Biggers, penned *The House without a Key*, and introduced the world to the fictional Honolulu detective, Charlie Chan. On February 1st, 1927, in between the Moana and the Halekulani, the Royal Hawaiian Hotel opened its doors and became the in place for Hollywood stars and international royalty.

Now, 80 years later, all the participants in *The Massie Affair* are long dead. However, the racism and duplicity entwined in *The Affair* linger on and remain as ghostly shadows that haunt our Land of Aloha.

The author of *Ena Road*, Dennis M Keating, relocated to Honolulu from Chicago nearly 50 years ago. His life in Honolulu, has indirectly been tied to Ena Road. Initially, in 1969 he resided very near Ena Road. Later, he moved on. First, across the island, then, quite literally around the world to the US mainland, Germany, Thailand and then China.

In 2002, after years of travel, Keating returned to Honolulu, again. And once again, his home is just off Ena Road. Because of this proximity and his love of Honolulu, *The Massie Affair* has fascinated his curiosity.

Did little Ena Road
cause Joe to die?

Yes, but only
because of a lady's lie.

Ena Road is just
300 yards long.

Joe was Hawaiian,
young, healthy, and strong.

In truth, he was downed
by a .32 slug,

Fired with hate

by a crazed, hate filled thug.

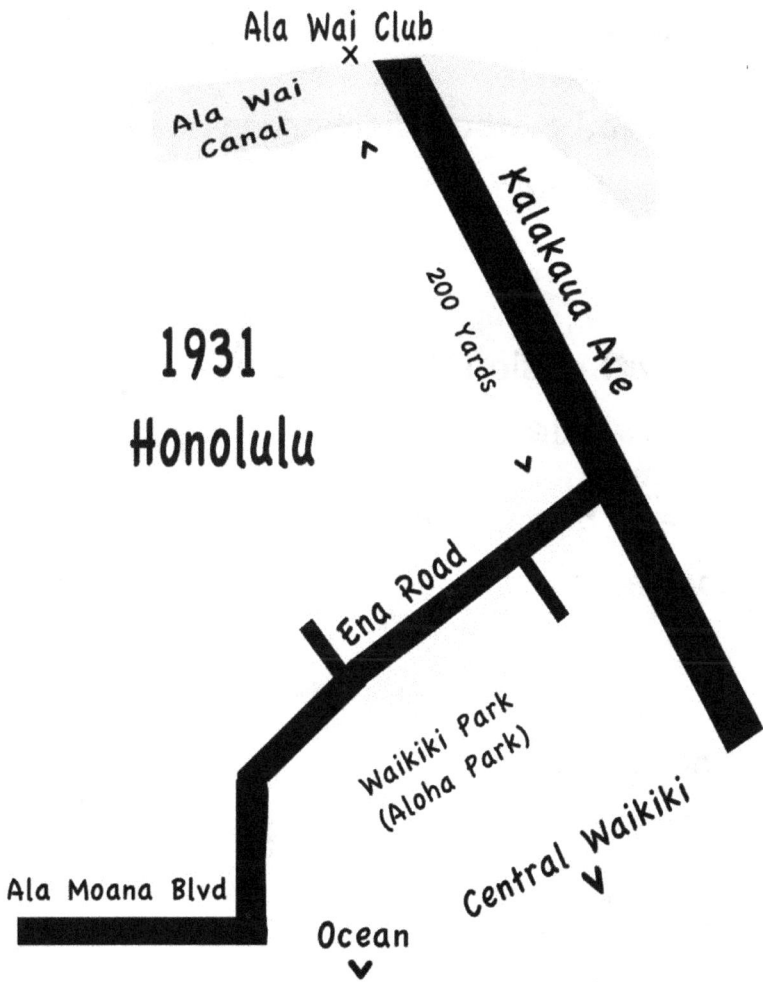

Ala Wai Club
×

Ala Wai
Canal

Kalakaua Ave

200 Yards

1931
Honolulu

Ena Road

Waikiki Park
(Aloha Park)

Central Waikiki

Ala Moana Blvd

Ocean

A small .32 slug?
Does that seem strange?

Not really, when discharged
at close range.

Thalia Massie is at the crux
of this tale,

A teen bride, in a marriage
doomed to fail.

She had mental issues
despite being pretty.

To be truly fair,
she deserves our pity.

Ena Road, a minor street on the downtown end of Waikiki, links Kalakaua Avenue and Ala Moana Boulevard. During the 1930's, it housed several small family run shops and restaurants. Also, on the left side, about half way down, there was an amusement park known as Waikiki Park. The park had caravel rides, a penny arcade and a dance hall. It catered to low income Honolulu locals rather than affluent tourists.

In 1928, the dredging of the Ala Wai Canal was completed in order to drain the rice paddies and turn Waikiki into a tourism playground. Waikiki is rectangular. On two sides, it is held in by the Ala Wai Canal. The third side faces Kapiolani Park and the fourth side fronts the ocean.

Thalia's banal husband
left many in doubt.

His ticket to Annapolis?
Won by family clout.

A low-ranking officer
in the Hawaiian fleet,

His success plan:
Lick everyone's feet.

For sure, Thalia got punched
on Ena Road.

Perhaps, it was payback
for a previous goad.

Thalia Massie was Born on St Valentine's Day in 1911. At age 16, on Thanksgiving Day, 1927, she married a Navy Lieutenant. Then, at age 52, on Independence Day eve, 1963, she overdosed and died. Despite her ties to America's festive days, Thalia was a lonely person who simply never really fit in. She often defied society and, in general, she looked down upon others. Her rebellious acts often seemed to be tied to her personal frustrations, uncertainties and insecurities.

She seemed to detest her privileged life in Washington D.C. and Honolulu. While she disliked being a Navy officer's wife, she seemed to enjoy over indulging in alcohol and getting smashed at parties. Often, she sounded off loudly and rudely insulted others. Unsurprisingly, many Navy wives did not enjoy her companionship.

The culprit?
Probably, a navy man.

She had insulted more than a few
from that clan.

She had berated her spouse
and others shortly before,

Quite likely, one of them
chose to even the score.

Angry and upset, she'd stomped
from the Ala Wai Inn.

Did a sailor follow,
with hopes of sin?

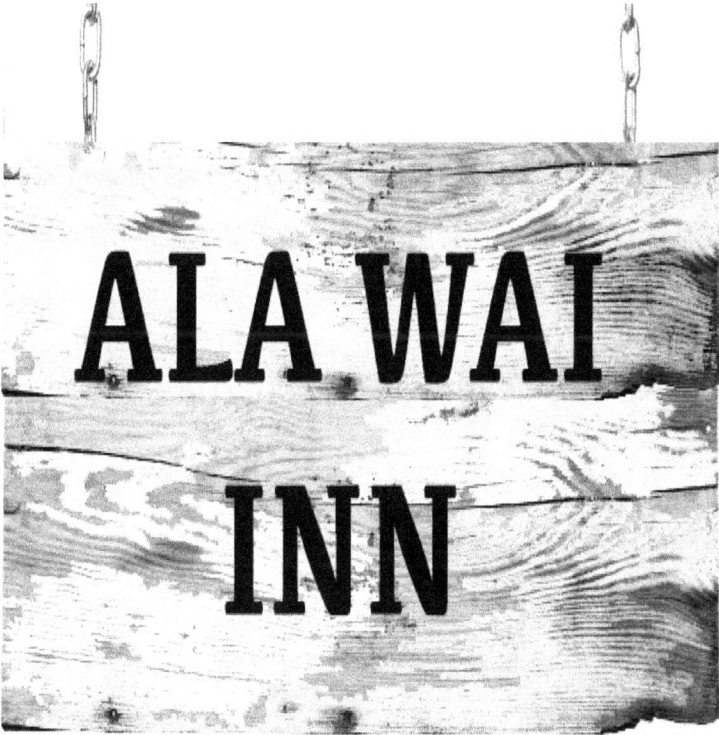

She was found "disheveled"
just off Ena Road.

Her speech tearful,
stuttered, and slowed.

Naturally, everyone thought
the worst case;

Due to her broken jaw
and her bruised face.

Upon examination,
the medics agreed,

She'd suffered a violent,
brutal deed.

The Ala Wai Inn was a restaurant, club and dance hall during the early 1930s. The Inn was located just across the Ala Wai Canal from Waikiki, near the location of the current Hawaii Convention Center, and near the corner of Kapiolani Boulevard and Kalakaua Avenue. On Saturday evenings, the Ala Wai Club was pretty much taken over by the US Navy. If Navy personnel wanted to meet up with each other, this was the place they chose.

But other nastiness
she had escaped.

The doctors concurred.
She had not been raped.

Everyone sympathized.
She was such a pitiful sight.

They didn't take note, how
her story changed during that night.

She blamed five local boys,
but others came to say,

When she was beaten,
those boys were miles away.

Navy Lieutenant Thomas Massie was a graduate of the U. S. Naval Academy in Annapolis, Maryland. In 1927, at age 22, shortly after graduation, he married 16-year-old, Thalia Fortescue. Back home in his small Kentucky town, Tommy was politically connected. He dreamed of making connections in Washington D.C. Thalia's father, a cousin of US President Teddy Roosevelt, had rode with Roosevelt's Rough Riders in Cuba during the Spanish American War. For Tommy, this was a political match made in heaven.

Tommy had been a so-so student at the Naval Academy and was proving to be a mediocre and unimpressive naval officer. Inside, he fully realized this. He knew his opportunities for advancement were tied to his being friends with everyone, especially those higher up the ladder.

For sure, Joe Kahahawai
was not in Waikiki.

Third-party testimony proved
he just couldn't be.

The only logical conclusion:
the lady chose to lie.

For this prevarication,
Joe was doomed to die.

Facts and timelines
were ignored by the naval elite.

Admiral Stirling, the Navy Poobah,
spoke for the fleet.

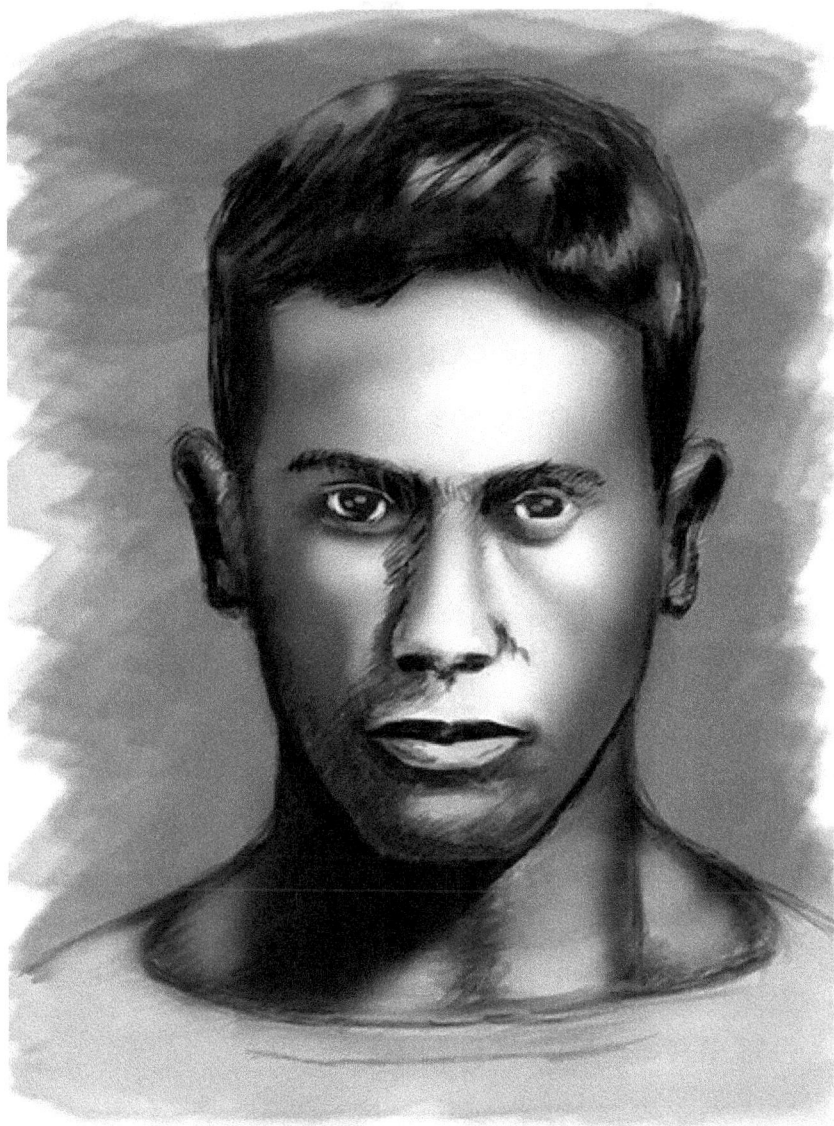

Joe Kahahawai

These brown-skins are savages.
Bring them to their knees.

Better yet, just get some ropes.
Hang 'em from the trees.

Thalia's mother? A self-styled
East Coast, Blue Blood.

Brown-skins were evil.
Navy men? Low-class scud.

Thalia, dazzled by her husband,
as a teenage lass;

Now, five years wiser, realized
he could only kiss ass.

The five young men accused by Thalia Massie:

Joseph Kahahawai - 20 years old

Ben Ahakuelo - 20 years old

Horace Ida - 24 years old

Henry Chang - 22 years old

David Takai - 21 years old

Thalia hated the Navy,
its fleet and its subs.

Her rude comments made her
unwelcome at navy wives clubs.

To Thalia, Oahu was
Just a lonely rock pile.

"How do I get off
this desolate isle?"

No surprise,
Thalia left the party alone.

Did a young sailor follow?
Someone she'd known?

Facts concerning Thalia Massie on the evening of Saturday, September 12, 1931.

Thalia and her husband, Tommy, joined other navy personnel at the Ala Wai Inn after having a few drinks at their home, three miles away, in the Manoa section of Honolulu. This was a regular thing for them, because Saturday evening was virtually Navy Night at the Ala Wai Inn. During the evening, Thalia and Tom, as usual, didn't hang out together. Thalia got into an argument with another navy officer and slapped his face. Later, after 11:00PM she left the Inn alone. She crossed the Kalakaua Avenue bridge behind the club and walked one block to Ena Road. It seems, some person on Ena Road, for some reason, slugged Thalia hard enough to break her jaw. The actual circumstance has never been determined.

Did his sensitive ear
lead to a sensual paw?

Did she yell, "Bug off!"
and he, then, smacked her jaw?

Maybe, Thalia slapped back
and he hit her again.

He then hurried off,
leaving her dazed and chagrin.

When her husband saw her,
he let out a shout.
She was injured, bloody,
and full of doubt.

Who slugged her? Her husband? She'd embarrassed him many times. Another Navy guy who followed her? Quite possible. A local guy on Ena Road? Also, possible. Only she and the assailant knew. That night, she changed her tale several times. Finally, it was, "This is my story. And, I'm sticking with it."

Her tale concerning the five local guys didn't hold water. She claimed she'd been dragged into the weeds and raped, yet her dress was neat and clean. The examining doctors stated she was not raped. Those five guys were involved in a traffic incident, three miles away, at the same time she was slugged. She'd read and heard police reports on the guys, before revising her story. The police reports included a license plate number and other details that she added to her tale.

If the truth showed
a navy man did this,

Rumors would fly. "Ooh là là!
Thalia's having a tryst."

She and her hubby would be dragged
through the dirt.

Better to claim those local savages
wanted under her skirt.

The police had picked up
five locals for another fight.

Blame these guys. Then the cops
would lock it tight.

Had a more thorough police investigation been done, the whole Massie Affair would have never occurred.

Forget that. We all know, sex, violence and the honor of white women sells newspapers. Add tales of jungle savages and the mysteries of the Pacific islands and every major newspaper in America pushed the story to the front pages.

The US mainland press followed the lead of the Honolulu papers and the Navy Commandant. They all came down 100% against the local defendants.

The national press chose to depict local Hawaii residents as uncivilized, jungle barbarians. The press and many national politicians advocated placing Hawaii under the rule of military marital law.

Logic and reason
flew over the wall.

White women's honor
became the Navy's battle call.

The military brass? "Hang, yes hang
these rapists for their deed."

The Honolulu newspapers?
"Guilty" in every lead.

Mainland media?
Jumped on the "Guilty" cause.

Jungle beasts deserve death.
They live without laws.

The US mainland press portrayed Hawaii as a lawless, uncivilized place.

When the case came to court,
the jury just viewed facts.

The prosecutor's case
was full of leaks and cracks.

Most jurors were local,
so the Haole elite cried foul.

"These brown-skins protect
each other!" they howled.

The Hung Jury verdict
shocked mainland USA.

"Lawlessness rules in
those islands far away.

Reflective the US press reports, the Kentucky House of Representatives on January 18, 1932 adopted Resolution H. R. 11, requesting that US President, Herbert Hoover, take action to bring Hawaii under martial law and make it safe for women. The resolution stated in part:

". In September last, the wife of Lieutenant Thomas Hedges Massie, an officer in the United States Navy and a native and citizen of Winchester, Kentucky, stationed at Honolulu in Hawaii, was kidnapped, assaulted, beat, mangled, her jaw broken and raped six times by five Oriental native Hawaiians, resulting in pregnancy, confining her to a hospital, and making an operation for abortion imperative. Although she identified four of the five rapists, the jury which tried them, failed to convict, leaving this foul and horrible crime unpunished. . ."

White women aren't safe
in that primitive place.

Dark-skins lack the morals
of our superior race."

The press, upper class,
and military spoke as one:

"All five are guilty.

God demands justice be done."

Thalia's mother pushed Tommy

into a devious plot.

"Thalia's honor's been trashed.
We must remove this blot."

Rear Admiral Yates Stirling was the powerful Commandant of the Fourteenth Naval District and top honcho at Pearl Harbor. He believed the five local men were totally guilty and did not let the facts get in the way of his opinions. He publicly proclaimed his position with numerous racist comments. His statements and his strong displeasure with the hung jury, encouraged the sailors under his command to take physical action against the accused men. His opinions set the tone for the positions taken by the local and national press.

"We know Joe Kahahawai
was the lead guy.

Force him to confess;
then all five will fry."

With a phony summons & rented car,

they grabbed Joe.

"Just stick a pistol in his gut.
Act fast. No one will know."

Joe was tied down and beaten
more than a bit.

To survive, Joe figured
"I gotta try to split."

In 1930, Hawaii's population of 370,00. The majority were Asians brought over to work the sugar cane fields. Caucasians were in the minority, but controlled the power structure. Most Caucasians, or Haoles, as they are referred to locally, resided on Oahu, in Honolulu. Most of the US military were also stationed on Oahu. Basically, Haoles controlled the political, economic and social structure of Hawaii.

The Haole establishment was eager to have the whole *Massie Affair* resolved as quickly as possible. Yes, there was a rush to judgment. The Haole Establishment believed of Thalia's inconsistencies and confusion of facts, was due to the traumatic experience she endured and not because she chose to misrepresent or fabricate events.

Joe lunged.
The gun fired hot lead.
Within seconds,
Joe hit the floor, dead.

"Better dump the body
out by Blowhole."
The police, tailing them,
halted that goal.

With a nude corpse in back,
their alibi was lame.

The henchmen gang
had no one to blame.

Thalia's mother, Grace Fortescue was a New York City socialite and a relative of Alexander Graham Bell of telephone fame. Grace had numerous political and social connections in New York as well as Washington D. C. When the Massie Affair started, she had immediately sailed to Hawaii to support her daughter. She then rented a home near her daughter's home.

Grace was the main protagonist in the planning, organizing and kidnapping of Joe Kahahawai. Due to her connections, back on the East coast, she was able to induce famed criminal lawyer, Clarence Darrow to come out of retirement and defend her and the other defendants in the murder trial.

This caused a second trial
in the Massie Case,

"Murder One!"
was the new charge to face.

Get famed lawyer, Clarence Darrow,
"He'll save the day."

No luck. Factual evidence
dwarfed what Darrow could say.

The jury and judge
decided once again.

"The haoles are guilty.
Ten years in the pen."

In 1931, Clarence Darrow, undoubtedly was the most famous lawyer in America. He had already been retired several years and was well into his 70's, when he was approached to take the Massie Case.

Apparently, Darrow took the case and came out of retirement for two reasons. One, due to the stock market crash of 1929 he had lost much of his savings. He was near broke and simply needed the money. Two, he had never been to the islands and Hawaii was on his bucket list.

Normally, Darrow chose to defend the downtrodden. This time, he threw in his lot with the establishment. It is interesting how money is often the guiding light of one's moral compass.

No way!
The white establishment cried "No!"

So, with one-hour house arrest,
Governor Judd let them go.

The killers partied
late that night.

Totally free,
they made jokes of their plight:

White man's purity
had saved them from jail.

Days later, to San Francisco,
they all set sail.

JOSEPH
KAHAHAWAI Jr
BORN DEC 25 1909
KILLED JAN 8 1932

Now, some eighty years have passed;
The players have met their fate.

The Massie Case is legend;
And Hawaii's now the 50th state.

As for poor Joe, his body lies
in Kalihi, under six feet.

Buried in Puea Cemetery,
just off School Street.

No surprise, Thalia's marriage
took a downward course,

It ended two years later
with a Reno divorce.

Aftermath - Thalia

At the Reno divorce court, Thalia told the press, she would never marry again. Later that evening, she went back to her hotel room and attempted a drug overdose. Both her attempted suicide and her plan to stay single were unsuccessful. In 1953, at age 42, Thalia did marry again. This time she chose a 21-year-old college student who had not yet been born when the whole Massie Affair started. No surprise, her second marriage was a short one.

Over the years, she tried to commit suicide numerous times. Finally, at age 52, her last suicide attempt was successful and her sad life ended.

With suicide concerns,
her family kept her close.

Then, in 1963, her sad life ended:
a drug overdose.

Today, Hawaii evolves,
mostly for the good.

Race issues are better,
not as ideal as they should.

True, the Massie Affair,

Happened many years ago,

But to truly know our islands,
It's something you should know.

Aftermath – Joe Kahahawai

Joe's Kahahawai was born Christmas Day, December 25, 1909 and murdered twenty-two years and two weeks later on January 8, 1932.

Joe, a Catholic, had attended St Louis high school through a football scholarship. He was an active athlete in other sports including boxing.

His funeral mass was held at the Lady of Peace Cathedral in downtown Honolulu. After the service, the pallbearers carried Joe's casket by hand, two miles to Puea Cemetery in the Kalihi neighborhood of Honolulu. There, a second service was held. It was stated that more than 1,000 individuals attended the service and that it was the largest funeral service since the death of Hawaii's last queen, Queen Liliuokalani, fourteen years earlier.

Aftermath - Tommy

Tommy fared little better than Thalia. He married again in 1937. While his second wife did not have psychological issues, she got embroiled in an international incident in Tsingtao, China a year after their marriage. After visiting Tommy aboard his ship, she returned to a pier where a Japanese sentry slapped her in the face for failing to comply with his Japanese language orders.

Unfortunately, Tommy's whole life continued to crumble. He began to show signs of psychiatric disorders. His condition got worse and prior to World War II the Navy decided to release him from active duty. Tommy lived until 1987, but his life was a sad and bitter one.

Aftermath – Grace Fortescue

Thalia's mother, Grace, orchestrated the whole plot to kidnap Joe Kahahawai. Unlike, Thalia and Tommy, the whole Massie Affair really never phased her.

Grace shrugged off her manslaughter conviction for killing an innocent man and returned to her socialite role on the East Coast. She was not shy to discuss, in her words, "the murder."

Two years after the Massie Affair, she inherited her full share of the Bell estate and bought a house in the Bahamas. She lived a full active life as a rich widow, well into her nineties. Thanks to her deceased husband's military service, this key plotter in Joseph Kahahawai's murder was honored by our nation and buried at Arlington National Cemetery.

The Ballad of Joe Kahahawai
A poem by Dennis M Keating
Copyright © 2017 Dennis M Keating

If you wish to accompany this poem with a guitar, recommend using a tune similar to
The Night They Drove Old Dixie Down
by Robbie Robertson

Joe Kahahawai was his name,
And he came from the Valley Isle.
While restless and untamed,
He won many friends with his warm smile.

The day they shot poor Joe down;
His killers were driven by hate.
The day they shot poor Joe down;
It changed our island's fate.
And we cried, "No, na, na, na, na, no."

Joe was just 22, proud and brave;
When that .32 slug laid him in his grave.
It was all due to the lady's lie
That Joe became an innocent fall guy.

The day they shot poor Joe down;
His killers were driven by hate.
The day they shot poor Joe down;
It changed our island's fate.
And we cried, "No, na, na, na, na, no.

It was January of 1932.
With one slug to his chest; Joe was through.
They'd kidnapped Joe near the courthouse;
They said to avenge a wronged spouse.

The night the lady cried, "Rape!"
All the whites were teeming.
The night the lady cried, "Rape!"
All the news headlines were screaming.
They screamed, "No, na, na, na, na no."

Back in Kalihi, Joe's mother cried.
She'd lost her hope, her dream and pride.
"Oh, dear God! Set me free!"
"My only son's been taken from me."

The day they shot poor Joe down
His killers were driven by hate.
The day they shot poor Joe down
It changed our island's fate.
We cried, "No, na, na, na, na, no."

"Now I don't mind my hotel job.
Sure, I kowtow to some mainland snobs.
While they talk down to me, at night I rest.
But God, why did you taken my very best."

The Day they buried Joe Kahahawai;
All the Hawaiians marched proudly.
The Day they buried Joe Kahahawai
All the women wailed loudly.
They wailed, "No, na, na, na, na, no."

The court told the killers "You're guilty!"
And gave them ten years in the pen.
But, Governor Judd said, "I'll make you free.
Just wait an hour and, you're on the street again."

The day they let the killers free;
It was Hawaii's death knell.
The day they let the killers free,
Was the day, Hawaii's soul went to hell!
We all cried, "No, na, na, na, na, no."

The
Fulda Gap

A Cold War Standoff

DEDICATION

To the Men and Women Who Defend Our Freedom

The Fulda Gap tells of the Cold War situation that existed in Germany from the late 1940's until 1990. *Fulda* is a small town in central Germany. The *Fulda Gap* is an open plains area that played a critical role during the tense Cold War. The Cold War ended with the destruction of the Berlin Wall, along with the 860 miles of landmines, barriers and guard posts that divided Germany from the Baltic Sea to the Czechoslovakia border.

In prior centuries invading army knew the Fulda Gap as the Hessian Corridor. During the Cold War, US Army soldiers of the 3rd Armored Division and other units stood eyeball to gun turret against the Soviet Block tanks. Our guys and gals where the first line of defense against the communist forces that sought to demolish Germany. During this perilous fifty years, the Third Herd took on the moniker, *Defenders of the Fulda Gap.*

Cold War: Inner German Border

West
Germany

Helmstedt

Berlin

East
Germany

Russian Tanks

Fulda

Frankfurt

Most people don't know
the Fulda Gap,

And couldn't find it
on a map.

It's located across
the Atlantic sea,

Smack dab in the middle
of Germany.

This open flatland,
half a world away,

Has been well traversed
since ancient day.

An American Sector sign, located near Berlin's Checkpoint Bravo, in English, Russian, French and German. To us, it meant, once you go passed this point, we cannot promise we can help you.

Its military significance
goes back to yore.

The Kaisers knew it
as The Hessian Corridor.

It's a wide plain that cuts

East to West.

Large armies can cross it

with ease and finesse.

Napoleon viewed the Gap

as a European main street

When his troops attacked Moscow,
then beat a fast retreat.

In 1812, Napoleon sought to place all of Europe under the control of France. With this goal, he sent the French Grande Armée to conquer Moscow. The campaign was a total failure that left Napoleon's military permanently crippled.

The Gap's character changed
after World War II.

You see, the Cold War
put Germany to the screw.

The old Vaterland
literally, was cut in half,

Like some evil demons
sliced it with a magic staff.

With this, central German towns

took on a border role,

And an East Bloc Commie monster
eyed them with evil in its soul.

Cold War: The half century of military and political hostility between the West and the Soviet Bloc.

Fulda: A small town in central Germany.

Fulda Gap: A central Germany lowlands area that is very suitable for the swift movement of military troops and tanks.

Hesse: A federal state in the Federal Republic of Germany.

Vaterland: German for Fatherland.

East Bloc: The group of communist states located in Central and Eastern Europe that were virtually under the control of Russia from after World War II until December 26, 1991, the day the USSR (Union of Soviet Socialist Republics) was officially dissolved.

Commie: A Communist, mainly a Soviet.

The town of Fulda
became the crosshair place,

Where soldiers on both sides
stared, face to face.

If Russian tanks were to attack,
there's no doubt

The lowland openings near Fulda
would be the route.

West Germans knew this probability

to be very great.

They'd studied Cold War history well.
And could only to sit and wait.

Soviets: Member of the former Russian controlled USSR (Union of Soviet Socialist Republics).

In the Fall of 1956, Soviet military and tanks invaded Hungary and its capital, Budapest.

Ivan: Common Russian name that became a nickname for a Communist or a Soviet.

Ruskie: Nickname for Russian.

In the Summer of 1968, Soviet military and tanks invaded Czechoslovakia and its capital Prague.

Klick: Slang for kilometer. Ten kilometers or klicks equals 6.2 miles.

Willkommen: Welcome in German.

ICBM: Intercontinental Ballistic Missile.

SAC: US Air Force Strategic Air Command.

In the 1956 attack on Budapest,

2,500 of Ivan's tanks led;

Three days later,

20,000 Hungarians lay dead.

Then, 2,000 Ruskie tanks
moved on Prague in '68,

The Czechs quickly surrendered
to avoid the same fate.

What options could
the Allied generals weigh?

All of West Germany was

Just a few hundred klicks away!

Cold War: Beginning and End

The war in Europe ended with the surrender of Germany on May 7, 1945. During the next two years, the Soviets, under Stalin, continued a policy of geopolitical aggression. On March 12, 1947, President Truman stated enough is enough. He announced the US would begin to counter the Soviets. This day is viewed as the day the Cold War started.

On November 9, 1989, the Berlin Wall was breached. This was not the end of the Cold War. While the opening of the wall was a very major incident, it was just one event in the whole domino process. Officially, the Cold War ended on December 26, 1991, when the USSR or Soviet Union totally broke apart, dissolved, and ceased to   exist.

Please see Cold War Timelines at end of this poem.

Should a massive tank charge
plow through,

West Germany'd be flattened
in a day or two.

With armies fighting,
not only soldiers would die;

The civilian body count
would also be quite high.

When would the attack occur?
Well, Moscow held that ace.

We just knew, when it came,
Fulda would be the place.

A US M60 Tank

The NATO plan,
you may not want to hear

For the Allied bosses moved
the German troops to the rear.

At each Fulda fence post
stood an American GI.

Yeah! Right up front! Our guys
were to be the first to die.

"Willkommen in Deutschland!
Enjoy your stay.

Hope a tank won't roll over you

before next Tuesday!"

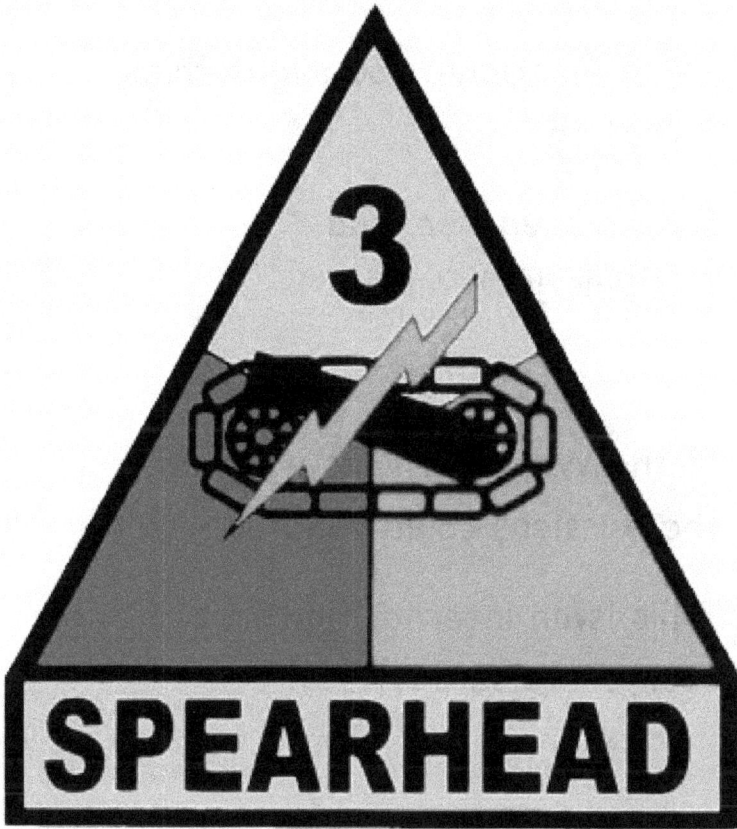

The insignia of the US Army 3rd Armored Division, sometimes referred to as the Third Herd. During the Cold War, they were **The Defenders of the Fulda Gap**.

As an American, you might think,
"What the hey?"

Take a breather, bud.
This was just Part A.

If the West Germans were up front,
the Russians could shout,

"This is an internal fight.
Everyone else butt out."

But with Yanks taking the lead,
the US would say,

"If you kill one of our guys.
Big time, you're gonna pay."

Cold War: The City of Berlin

There is a misconception that Berlin was a border city during the Cold War. This is incorrect. Berlin was located some 110 inside Communist held East Germany. Berlin was totally encircled by East Germany. West Germany had two boundaries: the 850-mile barrier that separated West and East Germany; and the 96-mile wall that encircled Berlin.

At the end of World War II, Berlin was divided into four sectors overseen, respectively, by the British, French, Americans and Soviets. The three western powers cooperated and their sectors melded together. The Soviet sector linked with East Germany. On June 24, 1948, the Soviets blockaded all shipments into West Berlin. The Soviet goal: Starve to death all the West Berliners. The Allies countered this plan with the Berlin Airlift.

Part B of our plan came from Alaska,
Our 49th state,

It concerned our heavy hitters,
who could seal Russia's fate:

An ICBMs and long-range bombers mix,
courtesy of SAC.

They packed nuclear warheads.
A real and frightening fact.

Our Alaskan bomber wing planes
were always in the air.

Of this, the Kremlin leaders
were keenly aware.

Map of Cold War Berlin

East Germany

Berlin

French

British

Soviet

X
Checkpoint
Charlie

USA

X
Checkpoint
Bravo

Autobahn
to West
Germany

If USSR tanks rumbled thru Fulda,
on any given day,

Our missiles were already locked on
Moscow just four hours away.

This chilly standoff played out
for forty long years.

Both sides were tense, but they hid
their private fears.

Whenever I ventured near the fence,
I held a certain dread.

If a young Russian soldier screwed up.
then Blam! Blam! Everyone's dead.

Cold War: Orders for Travel to Berlin

We military-related Americans needed **Movement Orders** documents when driving through East Germany.

Note the **Movement Orders** and their dates on the next page. The **Orders** are in Russian, English and French, and have Russians approval stampings. Yes, the Russians had total control over East Germany; and did so, for a couple years after the Berlin Wall went down.

When we traveled by car, the American Military Police always cautioned us: Don't drive too fast, nor too slow. Drive too fast and you give the Soviets a reason to arrest you. Drive too slow and you fail to arrive at the predetermined time. Then, the US Command presumes the worst and sends a helicopter to pluck you out of Ivan's hair and return you to Uncle's care.

Sometimes, with official orders,
I'd cross through the fences.

Each time I did,
it numbed my senses.

The East and West differences
were beyond rad.

When I returned home,
my heart was empty and sad.

Just a few steps thru the checkpoint
I'd start to mull:

Why is East Germany so dreary, desolate,
and dull?

Movement Order/Travel Document

UNITED STATES OF AMERICA
ÉTATS-UNIS D'AMÉRIQUE
СОЕДИНЕННЫЕ ШТАТЫ АМЕРИКИ

MOVEMENT ORDERS
LAISSEZ-PASSER
ПУТЕВКА

КПП Марийенборн

ВЪЕЗД

Name Nom, Prénom Фамилия, Имя	Rank Qualité Чин	Nationality Nationalité Гражданство	Identity Document No. Pièce d'identité No. № удостоверения личности
KEATING DENNIS M	Civ	American	NU 65,528A
JOHN THOMPSON	Civ	American	NY 66,653A
BOGHOS MICHAEL L	Civ	American	NY 66,949A

is / are authorized to travel from
est / sont autorisé(s) à se rendre de
уполномочен/уполномочены
следовать из   **Helmstedt**

to
à
    Berlin

and return
et retour
и обратно

by train or by vehicle No.
par le train ou par voiture No.
поездом или на автомашине №   **KD 7015**

from (date)
du (date)
от (числа)   **17 Feb 90**

to (date)
au (date)
по (числа)   **19 02 22 Feb 90**

inclusive
inclus
включительно

by
par

КПП Марийенборн

ВЫЕЗД

The Commander-in-Chief of the United States Army, Europe
Le Commandant-en-Chef de l'Armée Américaine en Europe
Главнокомандующим Американской Армии в Европе.

КПП Мозабос

ВЪЕЗД

Signature
Подпись

Title
Qualité
Звание   RONALD J. SUTHERMAN
Lieutenant Colonel, Adjutant General
Assistant Adjutant General

Date
Число   **16 Feb 90**

HEADQUARTERS
OFFICIAL
U.S. ARMY, EUROPE

Document needed to travel through East Germany.

It's the same people, same families,

just a barrier fence apart.

But West Germany was prosperous;

the East was not.

Fortunately, this crazy powder keg
never did blow.

I feared the fuse might speed up!
But, it burned forever slow.

There were no tank attacks;
No fiery climax, nor a big boom.

Time just had its way of undercutting
the pending, certain doom.

Cold War: Travel to Berlin

When we drove to Berlin, our journey began at the Helmstedt border crossing, **Checkpoint Alpha**. From there, we took Bundesautobahn 2, for 110 miles, or 180 Klicks, until we got to **Checkpoint Bravo** the American entrance to West Berlin.

Driving through East Germany could be a bit unnerving, like when we encountered a soviet tank or troop carrier. For sure, we had to stop at a few foreboding East German checkpoints. Sometimes, the checkpoint guards hassled us. At other times, they wanted to swap black market goods for money. Were these legit offers? Or, were we being set up for a sting? To me, indefinite lodging in a Soviet cell didn't sound cool, so I forewent the offers and never found out. In hindsight, I preferred flying from Munich to Berlin's Tempelhof airport. It was more relaxing.

It took four decades for the Commie

Façade to wear thin;

Corruption and stagnation ate
the Soviet Union from within.

Finally, in 1989, the Berlin Wall

came tumbling down,

Freedom, joy, and peace became
the new game in town.

Those involved felt great relief

from the Cold War strain;

And very few have an interest

In doing a replay, again.

Cold War: Checkpoint Charlie

The famous **Checkpoint Charlie** was used when going from West Berlin into Soviet Controlled East Berlin. When driving alone, **Charlie** could be a very harrowing Checkpoint. First, upon entrance, an East German soldier would thrust a Kalashnikov at my face. My orders: ***Don't roll down the window. Just show your Travel Orders through the glass.*** After a few moments, the guard would back down and lower his weapon.

Then, after maneuvering my auto through several concrete barriers, two Russian tanks greeted me. The tanks would adjust their gun turrets so that they aimed directly at my front windshield. Then, after a few moments I was waved though.

Believe me, I always felt great relief, upon my return to West Berlin, when I saw our Stars and Stripes flying in the breeze.

While the Fulda Gap fence isn't
as well known as the Berlin Wall,

To those trapped inside,
that fact meant nothing at all.

For them, both barriers
were visible to see,

And both existed to keep
those inside, other than free.

Sure, this crazy period ended,
More than twenty-five years ago

But due to its impact on our world
It's history that's good to know.

Old Glory

When one travels throughout the world and encounters hotspots and challenging situations, it is always refreshing to come upon our Red, White and Blue flying high over one of our embassies, consulates or military installations.

Background: Pre-World War II

For several centuries, Europe consisted of kingdoms, big and small. Due to changing alliances, invasions and military actions, the various boundaries frequently shifted and changed.

World War I ended with the Treaty of Versailles. This resolved many matters, but also created new ones. Naturally, the winners wrote the treaty for their advantage, while the losers, mainly, the Germans, were left with bitterness. A decade later, Hitler would build a power base that drew upon the festering wounds felt by his countrymen.

Meanwhile, Poland and other countries were caught between the super powers of Germany and Russia. Poland became a punching bag with its shape being continually transformed by its neighbors.

The author at the Berlin Wall. With sledge hammer in hand, he had the distinct personal pleasure of participating in the destruction of the Berlin Wall. He still keeps his souvenirs.

Cold War Background: Adolph Hitler

1889 Apr 20 Hitler born in Austria, across the river from Germany.

1914 Jul 28 World War I starts; Hitler joins the Bavarian Army.

1919 Sep 12 Hitler joins DAP Workers' Party and becomes popular orator. Within six months, the DAP becomes the Nazi party. Within two years, Hitler becomes leader of Nazi party with his Make Germany Great Again rallies.

1923 Nov 11 Hitler arrested for high treason after failed Beer Hall Putsch where he attempted to overthrow the government. While in prison, Hitler writes *Mein Kampf*.

1933 Jan 30 Hitler is German Chancellor.

1934 Aug 02 Hitler becomes **Der Führer**.

Cold War Background: Joseph Stalin

1912 Jan 01 Vladimir Lenin founds the Russian Communist Party.

1917 - 1918 Lenin's communist forces overthrow the Czarist government of Russia. Within a few months, Lenin has the Czar, his wife and children executed.

1922 Apr 03 Stalin rises to Party General Secretary developing strong power base.

Dec 30 The USSR (Union of Soviet Socialist Republics) is formed. It grows to 16 republics with Russia at the helm. A sickly Lenin becomes the Top Banana, but Stalin starts taking major power grabs.

1923 Mar 09 Lenin has massive stroke.

1924 January 21. Lenin dies. Communist Party infighting intensifies with the two main players being Stalin and Trotsky.

1928 Jan 31 Stalin exiles Trotsky. Within a year, Stalin takes total control and becomes absolute dictator. Trotsky, goes on the run, relocating from country to country with Stalin Hit Squad keeping tab. In August 1940, Trotsky is assassinated.

1929 Dec 29 Stalin speech attacks the Kulaks, the wealthier farmers, signaling the start of Stalin' brutal Reign of Terror. Over the next two decades, many millions will be executed or forced into forced labor camp Gulags.

1932 Nov 09   Stalin's wife's suicide.

1941 Jun 22 Hitler launches **Operation Barbarossa**, bombing Soviet controlled Poland and sending troops to attack Russia. Stalin is forced to refocus and fight Hitler's troops. The German-Soviet part of World War II begins.

1953 Mar 03 Stalin dies.

Cold War: Soviet Power

There are recurring questions concerning how the Soviets obtained so much control and unbridled power over East Germany and Eastern Europe during the forty years of the Cold War. Much of this answer can be tied to the Tehran Conference in 1943 and the Yalta Conference of 1945. Many historians believe, at these conferences, the Soviet leader, Joseph Stalin, simply bamboozled, snookered and outfoxed the American leader, Roosevelt, who was too vain, ignorant and naïve to understand the long-range goals of the Soviets. While historians may disagree, the reality is, these two conferences played a major role in sentencing to death and/or long term slavery like conditions, innumerous peoples in both Eastern Europe and East Germany. A Cold War chronology follows.

Cold War Background: World War II

1936 Oct 25 Germany & Italy form Axis. Nov 25 Germany Japan Pact to fight USSR.

1939 Sep 01 Germany, under Hitler, invades Poland starting World War II.

Sep 03 Britain, France and others declare War on Germany.

Sep 17 Russia invades Poland.

1940 Sep 27 Japan joins Axis.

1941 Jun 22 Germany attacks Russia. Dec 06 Germany is pushed back from attack on Moscow (USSR).

Dec 07 Japan attacks Pearl Harbor. USA enters war, greatly expand World War II.

Dec 11 Germany declare war on USA.

1942 Apr 18 Doolittle Raid. US B-25 bombers attack Tokyo. The raid is a morale booster and sends a "Remember Pearl Harbor" to Japanese leaders.

1943 Nov 28 **Tehran Conference** (Churchill: Great Britain; Roosevelt: USA; Stalin: USSR) Held at Soviet Embassy. Roosevelt stays in a Stalin provided room, that is probability (99.9%) bugged.

1944 Jun 06 **D-Day** USA, Britain and Canada invade the European mainland at Normandy, France to repel the Germans. Jul 25 Allied Forces breakthrough Normandy and start to move forward. Aug 20 Allied troops enter Paris.

Oct 27 The 442nd Infantry Regiment is ordered to rescue the trapped Texas *Lost Battalion* near the German border. The all Japanese-American 442nd, starts with 4,000 men. It outfights strategically and numerically superior enemy forces with its Hawaii pidgin *Go For Broke* spirit and goes on to become the most decorated unit in the history of American warfare. The 442 earned 9,486 Purple Hearts and 21 Medals of Honors.

Dec 16 Germany's last major offensive, the *Battle of the Bulge* begins.

World War II Ends - Cold War Begins

1945 Jan 15 Allies advance on Berlin. Hitler relocates his headquarters to the Führerbunker, an underground bunker. Feb 04 **Yalta Conference** - Codename: *Argonaut.* (Churchill, Roosevelt and Stalin). Again, Stalin controls the show. Feb 13 Allies firebomb Dresden. Mar 09 US firebombs Tokyo. Probably, the deadliest bomb attack in history. April 12 Roosevelt dies. Truman becomes US president.

April 20 Hitler celebrates 56th birthday as Soviet forces encircle Berlin. April 29 Hitler marries his longtime girlfriend, Eva Braun. Americans liberate Dachau Concentration Camp near Munich. April 30 Hitler and his new wife start their honeymoon by committing suicide. May 01 A German general negotiates a surrender of Berlin to Soviets. May 02 Soviets capture the Reichstag, Germany's capitol building and raise Hammer & Sickle flag atop the roof.

May 07 Germany surrenders to Allies. V-E Day (Victory in Europe Day)

June 05 Germany is divided into quarters, (American, British, French and Soviet.) July 17 **Potsdam Conference** (Churchill, Stalin and Truman). Potsdam, a suburb of Berlin. Goal: to settle World War II matters. Churchill is replaced by Clement Attlee due to British election. Truman, unlike the fawning Roosevelt and with A-bomb plan up his sleeve, matches Stalin's poker face resolve. Stalin cannot bully Truman, nothing is settled.

Jul 26 With the **Potsdam Proclamation** Truman tells Japan: Make an immediate unconditional surrender or face "prompt and utter destruction." America drops pamphlets on Japanese cities warning of more bombs to come.

Jul 28 Japan ignores Truman with a screw you, Mokusatsu (kill it with silence) reply.

Aug 02 Potsdam Conference Ends.
Aug 06 Americans drop Little Boy on Hiroshima killing 70,000 Japanese.

Aug 08: Japanese leaders don't surrender. Stalin declares war on Japan.

Aug 09: Americans drop Fat Man and kill 80,000 in Nagasaki, Japan.

Aug 09 After six years of neutrality, Soviet troops invade Japanese held Manchuria.

Aug 10 Japan gives in and accepts Potsdam unconditional surrender terms.

Aug 15: V-J Day (Victory over Japan Day.)

Aug 24 Soviet Soldiers march into Korea. Sep 02 Japan officially surrenders aboard battleship USS Missouri in Tokyo Harbor. Soviets end 24-day war with Japan.

Dec 31 12:00 noon. **Proclamation 2714**. World War II officially ends.

1946 Feb 08 Kim Il-Sung becomes boss of Soviet Controlled (northern) Korea.

Feb 09 Stalin declares war is inevitable due to the dissimilarities of communism and capitalism.

Mar 05 Churchill's "Iron Curtain" speech.

The Cold War

The Cold War was a West (USA, NATO and its allies) verse East (Russia, the USSR and other communist states) standoff that began at the end of World War II and did not end until the USSR dissolved in 1991. While it impacted the world, Germany often proved to be the playing field.

1947 Mar 12 Truman announced US is prepared to counter the ongoing Soviet geopolitical aggression.

Jun 05 US announces Marshal Plan

1948 Feb 21 Czechoslovakia. Overthrown by Soviet Supported Communist forces. Jun 18 US, Britain and France agree on a common currency, the Deutsche Mark, for Germany. USSR says "No." This in effect establishes West Germany.

Jun 24 Soviets blockade Berlin.

Jun 25 Berlin Airlift begins.

1949 Apr 04 Creation of NATO.

May 12 USSR ends blockade of Berlin. The Berlin airlift continued in order to build up a sufficient stockpile of goods so that the city could function as normal.

Aug 29 Soviets explodes Nuclear Bomb. Sep 30 Berlin Airlift ends. Last plane carries two tons of coal for the winter. Oct 01 People's Republic of China established under Mao Zedong. Oct 24 United Nations established.

1950 Jun 25 Korean War begins with North Korea invading the South. Sep 15 US forces land at Inchon to counter North Korea.

1953 Jul 27 Korean Armistice signed.

1960 May 01 USSR missile shoots down Gary Powers' U-2 spy plane. Powers is taken prisoner.

1961 Apr 17 Bay of Pigs Invasion in Cuba. Aug 13 Just after midnight, East Germany seals border with West Berlin and begins construction of the Berlin Wall preventing East Germans to entry West Berlin.

1962 Feb 10 U-2 Pilot Powers released and swapped for a Russian spy at Berlin's Bridge of Spies (Glienicke Bridge).

Oct 16 Cuban Missile Crisis US halts Russian missiles plan.

1963 Jun 23 US President Kennedy visits West Berlin and, gives his famous *Ich Bin Ein Berliner* speech.

1964 Aug 02 Vietnam Gulf of Tonkin Incident, causing large scale US troop involvement in the Vietnam war.

1975 Apr 30 Saigon falls and the US exits Vietnam.

1985 Mar 11 Mikhail Gorbachev becomes top dog in the USSR. Between Stalin and Gorbachev there were five other leaders. Gorbachev realizes he has inherited a bloated, corrupt and highly inefficient bureaucracy. To counter this reality, he introduces Perestroika (restructuring) and Glasnost (openness) and decides to end the economic aid to Soviet satellites and open a way for them to break away from the USSR.

1986 Apr 26 Chernobyl nuclear disaster. Dec 26. Riga, Latvia. Early morning, after attending a rock concert several hundred youths march downtown shouting *Soviet Russia out! Free Latvia!* This incident causes waves of unrest throughout the USSR as youths in the other soviet satellites were inspired to demonstrate against Russia.

1987 Jun 12 President Reagan, in front of the Brandenburg Gate and the Berlin Wall gives his famous, *Mr. Gorbachev, tear down this wall* speech.

1989 Aug 19 Hungary opens border to Austria and allows 13,000 East German tourists to escape to the West.

Nov 09 Berlin Wall breached and East Germans can move freely into the West.

1990 May 04 Latvia gets independence from USSR. Other republics follow suit.

Oct 03 The two Germany's are reunited.
Oct 15 Gorbachev gets Nobel Peace Prize.

1991 Dec 26 Soviet Union dissolved and the Cold War basically ended. Game over. The Good Guys Won. Everyone go home. The various American military units and the Department of Defense activities began a serious review and phase down of all their European Operations.

1992 Jan 21 Four weeks later, the author, at age 51, was offered early retirement. offer. He knew his job was done. There was nothing more to do. It was time to move on. With a simple "Thank you and Auf Wiedersehen," he retired to a new life.

Thanks to his unique job circumstances during the last few years of the Cold War, the author was one of the few non-military authorized entry to every American military encampment along the East West German border. Prior to this, he had also been allowed entry to the top-secret SAC Control Center at McChord AFB in Washington state. The Control Center monitored our nuclear bombers as they headed toward Moscow. When the bombers reached the North Pole, the Control Center would order them to return to their base in Alaska. Immediately, another group would be instructed to replace them and directed to head to the North Pole.

The German government was very appreciative of the author's service in Europe. Upon the author's retirement, Germany offered the author full German citizenship; permanent residence; and a four-bedroom home in Munich at a very low rental rate. He kept his Munich apartment until 2005, thirteen years after his retirement. At that time, he chose to come out of the cold and return home to the warmth of Honolulu. The author continues to have a strong love for Germany and the German people.

East meets West at Berlin Wall opening

The author, Dennis M Keating, after breaking a hole in the Berlin Wall, shakes hands with an East German soldier.

Thank You
and
Auf
Wiedersehen

A

Chicago Tale

Murder in the City

DEDICATION

To the men and women who serve
and protect the city of Chicago

We Serve
And
Protect

Motto of the Chicago Police

Dennis M Keating joined the staff of the Superintendent of Police in the fall of 1965. He remained with the police for four years, until 1969. Keating was a civilian, not a patrolman. He did not wear a uniform nor carry a gun. However, his civilian staff position afforded him a very unique secondary seat in the inner circle of the Chicago Police leadership. This tale concerns one of his experiences during his four years with the Police Department.

To better understand the situation, during the 1960's, the Chicago Police Department underwent a major administration shift. This change was preceded by a police scandal that even by Chicago standards was too big to ignore. Due to this scandal, Richard J. Daley, the powerful mayor of Chicago, was forced to bring in an outsider, Orlando W. Wilson, to clean up the mess.

Wilson was not your ordinary police chief. He had a PhD in Police Administration, as well as a Harvard and Berkeley background. He also had one other feather in his hat. After World War II, Wilson oversaw the denazification of the German police. The skills he learned in post war Berlin served him well in rough and tumble Chicago. Wilson was given Carte Blanche freedom. Daley ordered the Ward bosses and Aldermen to keep their hands off. With this guideline, Wilson hired individuals based on their academic and intellectual abilities rather than their political clout. Many recent university graduates were hired into police headquarters. The building took on a fresher, younger look. The author was one of these newcomers.

In the Ghetto

In January 1969, Elvis Presley recorded the song, *In the Ghetto*. The song has a haunting beginning: "As the snow flies, on a cold and gray Chicago morning," and a tough conclusion: "an angry young man, face down on the street with a gun in his hand."

Three years earlier, in January 1966, on a cold and gray Chicago afternoon, young Donald Dean Jackson entered Fohrman Motors, a ghetto automobile dealership on the west side of Chicago. Jackson was carrying a concealed sawed-off shotgun. To the best of my memory, this is how it went down.

I'd joined the CPD
three months before,

My desk, a few steps
from the Old Man's door.

On the fourth floor
at the old 11th and State.

A pretty good job
with some political weight.

I'd married recently.
My wife, from out of state.

Twice, nightmares woke her.
Guns and death: a policeman's fate.

CPD – The Chicago Police Department, is the second largest, after New York City, non-federal law enforcement agency in the USA. The CPD has 12,000+ police officers and around 2,000 civilian staff.

The Old Man – Orlando W. Wilson, the Police Superintendent (1960 to 1967). Wilson moved his office out of City Hall, to get away from the politicians, ward bosses and aldermen. He relocated to the fourth floor of the building that housed the central police units that served the twenty-one police districts in the city. These central units included the crime lab, the communication center and the evidence room. This building's nickname came from the cross streets where it was located: ***11th & State.***

Wilson shared the Superintendent's suite with his top aides. In addition, Wilson's financial staff, including Keating, had offices in the suite.

I told her, "Don't worry,
I'm not a street cop.

No uniform. No gun. Just # 2 Guy
in the Finance Shop."

One day my boss waved me in,
As he's hanging up a call.

His face cold and emotionless.
That's all.

Staring at his desk,
he spoke in a solemn tone;

"Duffy, upstairs."
He pointed at the phone.

"Don't know the facts yet,"
he said.
"Jolene in Keypunch.
Her brother's been shot dead.

Go stay with her,
until it's all done.

Get her home safe.
Keep her away from everyone."

Jolene was sobbing loudly,
the other keypunchers all sad.

"I tried to stop him," she said,
"from turning bad!"

```
┌─────────────────────────────────────┐
│                                       │
│   Chicago Police Headquarters         │
│                                       │
│      1121 S. State Street             │
│                                       │
└─────────────────────────────────────┘
```

The Chicago Police Headquarters was located at 1121 S. State Street, from the beginning of the 1960's until the end of the 1990's.

Her tearful words
flooded across the room.

"I knew something terrible
would be his doom"

"Jolene, I'm sorry."
I spoke very low.

"Let's go next door
'til the detectives show.

They'll need a statement
from you.

I'll drive you home
when it's all through."

In the 1960's, the Chicago Police, like many organizations at the time, employed numerous keypunch operators, or keypunchers to enter data into the computers. The keypunchers at the Chicago Police Headquarters were located together in a large keypunch room. Most of the keypunchers were employees of the Computer Division. However, three keypunchers were employees of the Finance Division. These three keypunchers, of which Jolene was one, processed all the Police payroll data. Their leader reported to Keating.

Two detectives entered,
after a few minutes went by;

One questioned Jolene; the other
gave me the who, what, why.

Jolene's brother, Donald Dean Jackson,
had a long rap sheet.

An ex-con, six months out of Pontiac,
and back on the street.

 Jackson'd bought a new Caddy
for a thousand down;

Then hidden fees and high interest
made him drown.

Rap Sheet – Slang term used to describe a listing of an individual's criminal records.

An Ex-con – An ex-convict. Someone who has served time in prison for a criminal offense.

Pontiac - This notorious prison is located 100 miles south of Chicago. The Pontiac Correctional Center houses many of Chicago's worst Gangbangers. The 1973 and 1979 Pontiac Riots that killed both guards and prisoners were due to fighting between the Chicago street gangs.

Caddy - A Cadillac automobile. A popular set of wheels for ghetto pimps & hustlers during the 1960s.

"A Cadillac dealer
in a ghetto neighborhood."

Just those few words

didn't sound good.

He purchased the car

less than a month ago;

Each night, he went cruising

with a new bimbo.

On the street,
the Caddy was his tool.

Lookin' in its mirror,
"Oh God, I'm Mr. Joe Cool."

Chicago, as well as much of America, saw great economic growth and middle class affluence in the late 1940's and 1950's. Most homes had at least one television by the mid 1950's. There were many first-time home owners who chose to relocate to the suburbs of the city.

Fohrman Motors was an automobile agency on Chicago's Westside. Fohrman Motors had become quite well known during the early 1950's because of its aggressive use of local television advertising. During the late 1950's and early 1960's, many white families chose to move to the suburbs, and a white flight void was created. This void was filled by lower income black families and the Westside quickly transitioned into a black ghetto. Fohrman Motors lost its citywide popularity and became known as a ghetto automobile dealership.

Then, a fender bender;
the car needed minor repair.

  Mr. Cool's relation with the dealer went
ice cold from there.

He brought the car in
to get the fix-up done.

The salesman was curt.
"We have a problem, son."

"You don't get the car back
until more money's paid.

Read the contract's fine print.
That's how it was made."

Bimbo – A slang term for a young woman who appears physically attractive but is intellectually shallow.

Fender Bender – A minor traffic accident where the damage to the automobiles is minor.

Jackson flared inside.
"Fuck that shit.

You ain't gettin' a dime
til I'm driving it."

The standoff went on for several days.
Nothing was done.

Then Jackson walks in;
under his coat, a sawed-off shotgun.

"Hey, Mr. Salesman,
my car ready yet?"

"If you ain't got cash,
just turn 'round and get."

Fohrman Motors – 1960's era.

Location: 2700 W. Madison Street, Chicago, IL.

Fohrman Motors was founded in 1912 by Benjamin Fohrman the father of Sidney and Edward Fohrman.

With those words,
out comes the gun.

One quick trigger pull;
the salesman was done.

Seeing this, the two Fohrman brothers
bolted for the door.

Blam! Blam! Blood and guts flew.
Their bodies hit the floor.

Nearby, two robbery detectives
were cruising their beat,

They saw the car dealer employees
fleeing into the street.

Sawed-Off Shotgun - Normally the barrel of the shotgun is shortened to less than 18 inches and the stock is also shortened. This makes the shotgun easy to transport and conceal while affording much more powerful firepower than the normal pistol. These features make it a desirable weapon for big city criminals.

"The first shot from a sawed-off shotgun can cut you in half. The second shot can cut you into pieces. "– A Police Officer

Cruising their beat – Typically, police officers are assigned to patrol specific geographic areas of the city, these areas are called their beats.

Pulling their revolvers,
one made a quick guess:

"It's show time, partner.
Robbery in progress."

Detective Anderson took the front,
Detective Charles the side.

They hoped to circle the shooter

and leave him nowhere to hide.

Jackson fired at Andy,
then ducked to reload.

With this, Charles sprang
into fast-forward mode.

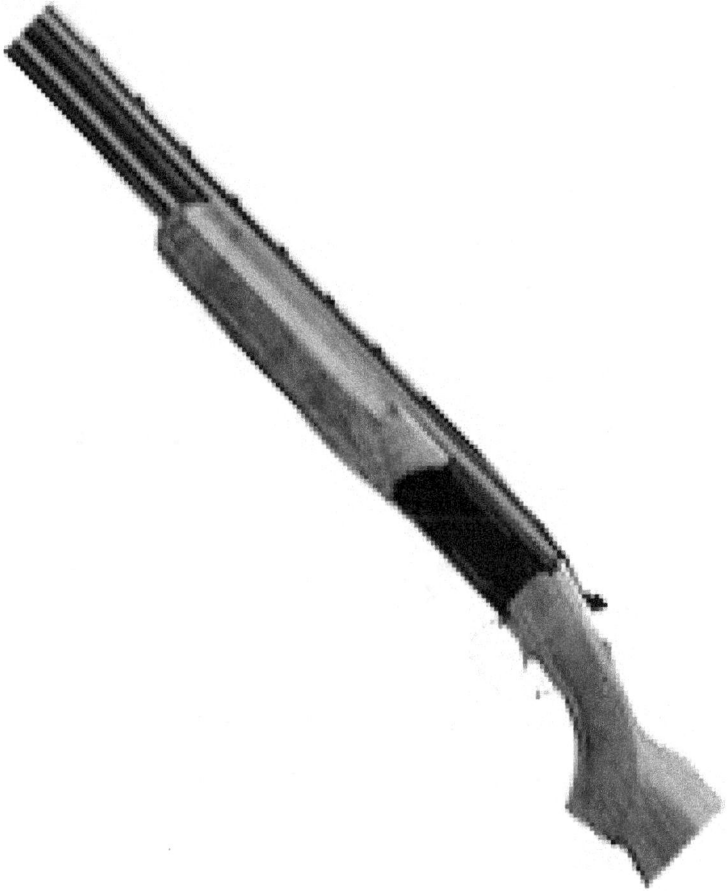

A Sawed – Off Shotgun

Charles, on the run,
shot his very best.

The first two slugs
went straight to Jackson's chest.

Then Charles emptied his .38
in the back of Jackson's head.

There was no doubt,
Donald Dean was 100% dead.

Charles nodded to Anderson;
all was through.

Once again, they'd covered each other.
That's what partners do.

A Police Snubnose .38.

A .38 can do the job, but it lacks the power
punch of a sawed-off shotgun.

Their adrenaline rushes subsided,
along with their fear.

Next, the paperwork. Then, a bar,
for quick shots chased by beer.

Back at headquarters,
the detective finished updating me.

"Now we go to the morgue.
We need a positive ID."

I looked at Jolene,
all swelled and teary eyed.

Gaining composure, she nodded,
she was ready to ride.

Cook County - The Illinois county where the city of Chicago is located. Cook County is the second most populous county in America after Los Angeles County and more populous than 29 of the 50 states.

Cook County Morgue - From the 1850s to the present day, the morgue has had a well-deserved, notorious reputation. for political patronage, unqualified and unskilled management, and a steady stream of lost bodies.

Political Patronage - Giving a job to an unqualified worker purely because he or she has a relative who has influence or connections. In Chicago, the term for political connections is "clout." Also, a common inquiry about someone's clout is, "Who's your Chinaman?" This is not a derogatory statement. Rather, it means, who is the unknown, behind the scene power broker, who got you your job?

The Old Cook County Morgue
was a disgusting place to go,

Nothing like a Crime Lab
on some CSI TV Show.

Once a Pre-Civil War hospital,
now, some hundred years old.

No upkeep money. All the jobs,
political patronage controlled.

The building's wooden entrance:
Dirty and grotesque.

Inside, an unshaven guy, chomping
a tamale at a cluttered desk.

Cook County Morgue

His food-stained shirt
appeared unchanged for a week.

He had a greasy, gooey glob
dripping down from his cheek.

His ear to a phone,
he was silent for a bit.

Then, suddenly, he barks,
"Stop your fucking shit."

"I don't know where the body is,
and don't give a rat's ass.

Tell your problem to the priest
next Sunday at mass."

Tamale – A popular Chicago snack of Mexican origin. At the time, tamales were often sold at street corner stands.

Coon – A derogatory, slang term for an African American

Ward Boss – For political purposes, Chicago is divided into fifty wards. The ward boss may be the elected alderman or the less visible behind the scenes, but very powerful, ward committeeman. Typically, in Chicago, virtually all the ward bosses are democrats and have control over patronage job appointments.

Hocker – Slang term for a mucus snot

Clipped - Killed

"I got a dozen unclaimed coons
lying in the basement vault.
If a couple got misplaced,
it ain't my goddamn fault.

Don't waste my fucking time
with your fuckin' loss.
If you don't like it, call my uncle.
He's the Ward Boss."

He had stared at us,
when we walked through the door.
Now, with an open-mouth cough,
he spits a hocker on the floor.

Three Fohrman Motors Employees

RIP – On January 7th, 1966
All killed by Donald Dean Jackson.

Albert Sizer, Age 64 – Salesman
Sidney Fohrman, Age 49 – Part Owner
Edward Fohrman, Age 42 – Part Owner

Shortly after the killing, the fifty-year-old Fohrman Motors dealership chose to permanently shutter its doors.

When he sees we're the cops,
he shrugs with a frown.

Then he stares at Jolene's breasts.
His tongue makes a clucking sound.

The detective was curt: "We wanna
see the guy the cops clipped."

The guy begrudgingly grumbles,
"Umph." Then he phones the crypt.

He tells us, "Cool your heels.
It'll be a little while.

Relax. Enjoy yourself, honey."
He leers at Jolene with a smirky smile.

Donald Dean Jackson

RIP – January 7th, 1966, Age 25
Killed by detective, Roland Charles.

The Fohrman Motors killings were covered by *Ebony* and *Jet*, two Chicago based magazines, whose primary market is the African American community. The January 27, 1966 issue of *Jet* reported that a Chicago alderman along with an Illinois state legislator were seeking to pass laws to protect citizens from usury loans with unreasonably high interest rates. The April 1966 issue of *Ebony* highlighted the Fohrman killings in an article on the pitfalls of credit buying, as it can hide inflated prices and extra finance charges. Seventeen years later, in 1983, the above-mentioned legislator won the election for Mayor of Chicago. His name was *Harold Washington*. He was Chicago's first black mayor.

Two more guys enter.
They look like the Press.

I nudge Jolene.
"We don't wan'em stirrin' up a mess."

"Go to the ladies' room.
I'll knock when it's O.K.

With luck, in ten minutes,
they'll go away."

The guy got the call from the crypt
a bit later.

By then, the Press left. I got Jolene.
We went to the elevator.

Shelf – The vault in the morgue where individual bodies are kept.

The day's events
kept spinning kinda weird.

All the time, I'm thinking,
"What am I doing here?"

"I've no interest in a bullet-holed
body," I thought to myself.
"I'll just stay at the elevator
and not go to the shelf."

No luck. The aide rolled
the body gurney across the floor.

White sheet on top, the cart sat
in front of the elevator door.

Detectives Roland Charles

RIP – December 19, 1974, Age 45
Nine years after the Fohrman killings

Detective Charles, a quiet and reserved man, received an award for bravery for his heroism at Fohrman Motors. He also received additional citations for other acts of courage. Detective Charles was an African American. Two weeks prior to his death, perhaps as a premonition of his coming demise, Charles wrote a three-page testament that included his belief that, "Mine is a wasted life." His letter focused on institutionalized racism and how it had limited him from his earliest days. His fellow police officers were shocked to learn of this as Charles was well liked and never expressed anger.

Jolene looked at the cart.
I stared at my feet.

"Is this your brother?" the aide asked,
pulling off the sheet.

One detective nudged Jolene.
She needed to confirm.

The poor girl stared, transfixed.
Her jaw very firm.

Then she grabbed my arm.
Her eyes opened wide.

"Dennis, look at his face.
He hadn't lied.

Detective York Anderson

RIP – September 15, 1985, Age 53
Eighteen years after the Fohrman killings

Detective Anderson, similar to Detective Charles, was also an African American. He also received numerous awards for bravery. He was a former US Marine Corps Sergeant who had been wounded during the Korean War. In 1970, he was put in charge of the first regular police patrol in the notorious Cabrini-Green Complex shortly after two police officers had been executed by a sniper. Some time after the Fohrman killings, the Chicago Police promoted him to Sergeant.

He made me a promise.
It's just like he said:

No worry, Sis. I'll wear a smile
when I'm dead.'"

Jolene's comments forced me
to take a look,

Though viewing a bullet-riddled killer
left me a little shook.

Sure enough, Jackson was smiling.
I swear on a case of bootleg gin.

He was staring up at me.
His mouth one big grin.

Chicago has long had the reputation of being the land of the gun. It gained its gangster notoriety during the prohibition days of the 1920's when rival gangs fought to bring illegal booze to the thousands of factory workers who yearned for a cold beer after a long day of hard work.

Unfortunately, Chicago continues to be known as a murder capital. In 2016, the city averaged two murders a day, with guns being the weapons of choice.

Though it was 50 years ago,
that day's still part of my life.

Thinking back, I hope Jolene
has had no more strife.

Now, it all bounces back into my mind,
when I hear that Elvis song play,

About a man shot down in a Chicago
ghetto on a cold and gray day.

Elvis Presley recorded the song,

In The Ghetto

on January 20th, 1969. It was released in April 1969. The song was written by the singer and songwriter, Mac Davis and was originally entitled, *The Vicious Circle*.

Many believe *In the Ghetto* played a significant role in Presley's 1969 return to popularity. Elvis died eight years later on August 16, 1977 at age 42.

As a young man
dies . . .
. . . another
baby child
is born
in the ghetto.

BLACK LAHU

Life and Death in the Triangle

DEDICATION

To the Hill Tribes
of
Southeast Asia

The Black Lahu are one of several Hill Tribes that lived in the mountainous areas of Southeast Asia. Their traditional lifestyles do not easily fit in with our way of life, nor our modern concepts of country borders and big city life.

Dennis M Keating first traveled to Southeast Asia in the early 1970's. Since then, his life has intertwined with the area.

In my youth,

I enjoyed adventurous tales,

Of jungle dangers

And smuggler trails.

Being fascinated

By intriguing scenes,

The Golden Triangle

Lit my radar screens.

So, it was, some

Six decades ago,

The Triangle's mysteries

I wanted to know.

THE GOLDEN TRIANGLE

I fixated on the Triangle
As a cool place to stray.

But then, life's realities
Got in the way.

School, family, job, and money,

All came first,

Before I could fulfill

My wanderlust thirst.

Gradually,
These issues got resolved.

Events unfolded.

My life evolved.

The Golden Triangle is the area in Southeast Asia that produces opium. The Black Lahu are one of the hill tribes living in the Golden Triangle.

In the Triangle, Burma, Thailand and Laos are the major opium trade players. China and the other neighboring countries play lesser roles.

While China is not normally viewed a as part of the Golden Triangle, my personal experiences in Chinese and Thai border towns motivates me to view China as a Triangle country. This said, Chinese history has been entwined with the opium business for hundreds of years; long before the Opium Wars of the 1800's. Also, the Chinese Diaspora to other Asian countries has often played a part in the opium trade. A Diaspora is the movement of a large group of people from their homeland to other countries.

Meanwhile, through books and maps
I'd glance,

Noting the four countries
In the Triangle's expanse.

Burma and Thailand
Are its main part.

They are the Triangle's
Soul and heart.

Laos and China round
Out the four.

These two shielded
Burma's back door.

The Gold in the Golden Triangle name relates to the income that is generated from the cultivated poppies. One reason concerns the fact that early Chinese traders used gold as their primary currency.

In general, the poor villagers in these remote areas have been subsistence farmers for centuries. They produced just enough food to maintain their small villages.

Long ago, the village farmers learned opium poppy seeds were the one item outside traders would eagerly buy from them. The extra money they earned afforded them opportunities to buy medicine and other things their local crops did not provide.

They play lesser roles,
It's true.

But they do provide
A protective glue.

I consider Burma
To be the Triangle's heart,

So, I chose Rangoon
As the place to start.

It took maybe a week,
Certainly, not more,

For me to learn I'd picked
The wrong door.

Rangoon Burma

Burma became an independent republic in 1948. Just like the Republic of Ireland three decades earlier, Burma chose to go it alone and break away from its former British overlords.

Since that time, Burma has had many honorable and well respected civilian leaders and many despicable and corrupt military leaders.

The local youths truly
Welcomed me.

All eager to learn of
The Land of the Free.

But when we talked
They kept a watchful eye.

Any passing stranger
Might be a Junta spy.

Big Brother cared,
I had no doubt.

Many eyes watched
Whenever I went out.

Burma – The former name of the country now known as Myanmar. Old timers who consider the military Junta despots to be illegal continue to call the country Burma.

Junta – A military group that takes power by force.

Rangoon – The main city and former capital of Burma.

US Marines – Since 1949, Marines have been deployed to US embassies around the world to protect our diplomats and classified information.

Old Corps – A former active duty Marine. Young Marines have deep respect for those Marines who went before them and served at a prior time in the Old Corps.

And my room was searched
Each time I left.

But my used rolls of film

Were the only theft.

Our embassy Marines befriended me.

I was Old Corps.

They chauffeured me round town,

And filled me in on the score.

All were Asian Americans,
Who our government chose.

When off duty, they blended well
In civilian clothes.

Asian Americans – At the more sensitive US embassies in Asia, our government tries to assign Asian American Marines. Often, they are called upon to drive embassy staff and their family to appointments or meetings. In these circumstances the Marines wear civilian clothes. As Asian Americans, they blend in and don't attract attention to themselves.

Laos - A communistic country that is tightly controlled by a military clique.

Vientiane - The capital city of Laos. It borders Thailand and is the major city of Laos.

Kickback – A bribe or payoff.

My pretty tour guide seemed eager

To be my special friend.

I felt a romantic relationship

Was her desired end.

Despite these positive vibes,

The Junta kept tight control.

Visa renewals were impossible,

Even with a kickback toll.

I nixed living in Laos.
It had more than one con.

Its only action place:
The dirty border town of Vientiane.

Kunming – The capital city of Yunnan Province in the southwest of China. Kunming is nicknamed the Spring City due to its year-round mild weather. In the early 1990's, due to its sparse population and wide streets, Kunming was a pleasant place to ride a bicycle.

Jinghong – The main city in the southern most prefecture in Yunnan Province. Although Jinghong is three hours from the border, it is the place where deals are brokered. Minority ethnic groups account for two thirds of the population. Several of these minorities, such as the Lahu, are cousins to the same groups in Northern Thailand.

When visiting some of the Buddhist temples in this remote region of communist China, it was interesting to note they had pictures of the King of Thailand on their walls.

Also, Laos limited visas

To little more than a week.

No renewals. Period.

No matter what you seek

I flew to Kunming a few times,

And then headed south.

But, the China - Burma border

Was a steel-locked mouth.

I bummed around Jinghong

For several nights.

The dingy backroom bars

Offered curious sights.

Jesus Christ Superstar Monks

In those places,
Playing darts and shooting pool,

Young Buddhist monks

Seemed to be the rule.

They smoked weed, teased bar girls, And downed straight booze.

They also sported sunglasses

And were handy with pool cues.

All the monks were trim,

Rugged, confidant, and cool.

They seemed to be grads

Of the Jesus Christ Superstar School.

Mule – Someone who is used by a drug smuggling gang to physically move the drugs between countries by carrying them on their person. In this case, the mules had a primary, full time job as drug smugglers. In other cases, in Southeast Asia, criminal gangs hire naive western backpackers to be their one-time mules.

The backpackers get paid in cash or plane tickets; enjoy the money; and the thrill factor they feel from being a one-time smuggler. Unfortunately, Bangkok's Bang Kwang prison is full of young backpackers who wanted to add a little more adventure to their travel itinerary. Moral: It is truly unwise to compete in activities where the military and police hold major stakes.

Twenty Kilos – Twenty kilograms. Twenty kilos is equal to 44 pounds.

H – One of the many nicknames for heroin.

Later, I learned their real job –

Drug smuggling mules.

Border guards give monks a free pass
without any rules.

These Superstars moved easily

From country to country,

With robes hiding 20 kilos of H,

That no one could see.

They traveled freely

Between Jinghong and Chiang Mai

With no other words

Than "Bless you," and "Goodbye."

Party Boss – Often, the Party Boss is the local Secretary of the Communist Party. He insures the Party has a steady revenue stream and gets its fair share of the various activities in town. More often, he also makes sure that he gets his very large personal piece of the action.

Often, small town Party Bosses are neither intelligent nor charismatic. They have moved up the ladder of success and obtained their positions through family connections or *Guanxi*. If you plan to spend any time in China you must learn the term, *Guanxi. Guanxi* is best described as political connections or doing a favor to a higher up in order to get him or her to do something for you.

A hotel tour guide advised,
"Best you meet the Party Boss."

Without his blessing
I could suffer a very serious loss.

"You and I are now partners,"

He said, "Welcome to town.

1st, give me US $10,000 up front.
Never write anything down."

After going through the Triangle,
Part by part.

I concluded Chiang Mai
Was the best place to start.

Chiang Mai

I had a backup plan,

Just to reduce any doubt:

The midnight train to Bangkok,

If things turn totally south.

Chiang Mai is at
the Triangle's southern tip.

From here, the entire world

Is an easy trip.

A fort-like old town

With a moat and walls,

Known for ethnic crafts

And night bazaar stalls.

Chiang Mai Map

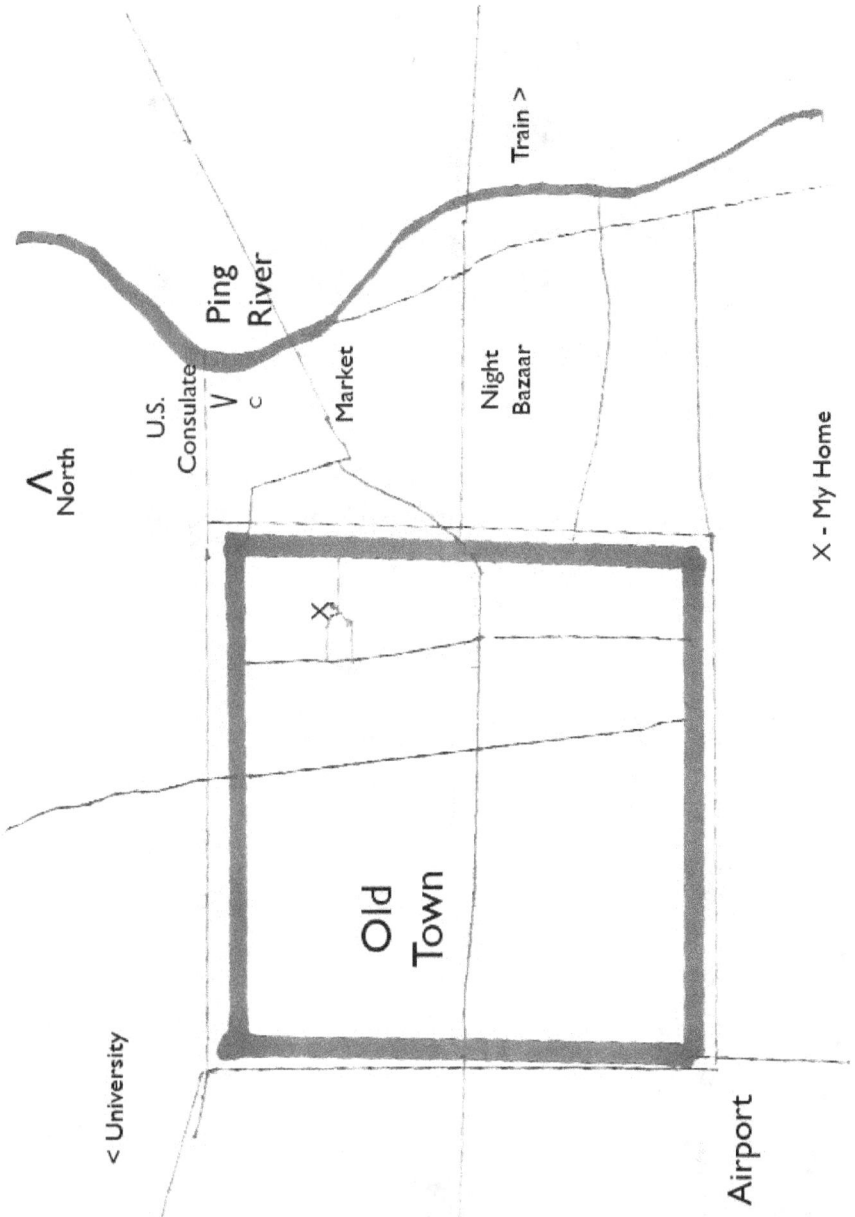

North

University

U.S. Consulate

Ping River

Market

Night Bazaar

Train >

Old Town

Airport

X - My Home

For Bangkok's middle class, there are

Many to-dos and must-sees,

Lots of family fun

And low-cost shopping sprees.

It offers Northern Thai cuisine,

Snacks and fruits,

And affords opportunities
To renew one's Buddhist roots.

Chiang Mai's also popular

With elderly Europeans.

The handicraft goods enhanced

Their travel scenes.

While Chiang Mai is the second largest city in Thailand after Bangkok, it is still a small town. Its population is only one-fifteenth the size of Bangkok.

Many of its inhabitants are countryside farmers who have moved into the city for better paying jobs. They have large extended families whose members continually gravitate back and forth between the city and the farm.

The Old Town has a square shaped outline. Each side having a length of about one mile. For romantic charm, a moat surrounds the old town and Buddhist temples dot the landscape. There is literally a temple on every block. You know you're not in Kansas anymore.

Buddhist – Thailand is a Buddhist country around 94% of the population is Buddhist

Throw in European restaurants with
Excellent German and French chefs.

The town scores high.
It's enjoyable and picturesque.

There are Buddhist temples

Wherever you face.

Tour books claim there are 300

In this small place.

Visitors enjoy

The town's easygoing feel,

Unaware of its ugly underbelly

That's very, very real.

French Chefs & Buddhist Temples

Twenty-somethings come here

For unique thrills:

Rafting, elephant rides,

And trekking in the hills.

The hostels are cheap

And very laid back.

"Relax. Enjoy. And guys, Um, maybe

You wanna buy some smack?"

Here's where the Triangle's

Details unfold,

And why people say

It's made of gold.

Wanna Buy Some Smack?

It's the poppy flowers

Growing just north of here.

They convert to heroin,

98+% pure.

As a young jarhead,

Stories were told,

Of flower-laced fields

Magically turned into gold.

G.I.'s tasted this forbidden fruit

During the Vietnam War.

It brought cheap nights of fun

And was easy to score.

Smack – Nickname for heroin.

Traffic - Unfortunately, in recent years, due to the increased number of automobiles, pickup trucks and motorbikes, Chiang Mai has lost much of its charm and has gained a few traffic jams. This has happened in many small towns in Asia. The main streets, that in the past served only the local townsfolk, have now become major thoroughfares for cross-country trucks and buses.

98+% pure – As the poppy flowers of the Golden Triangle are the source, the heroin available in the Triangle towns is as good as it gets.

Jarhead – Nickname for a US Marine.

G.I. – Nickname for US soldier.

During Nam, the draftees

Were 18-year-old guys.

Farm kids from Iowa and Nebraska

Learned to make buys.

Our young troopers were quick

To learn first hand

The joys and pleasures

Of exotic Thailand.

The Thai beachfront
was the fun place for R&R.

Pattaya Welcomes You!

Party time in every bar.

Pattaya

Fun City

Thai drugs, booze, and gals

Known for their smile.

They made this crazy Vietnam War

Seem almost worthwhile.

The '60's Hippy culture turned opium into a
world-class thing

As for processing poppy flowers,
North Thailand was the king.

Whether Palermo Mafioso

Or Hong Kong Triad Tong

For pure white powder,

You flew to CNX before very long.

R&R - *Rest and Recuperation*, or *Rest and Recreation*. (Your choice.)

Pattaya - A southern beach town two hours from Bangkok. Pattaya has a 24/7 party atmosphere and the reputation of being the Sodom and Gomorrah of Thailand. Pattaya got this reputation during the Vietnam War, when the American Forces started using the town for R&R.

During Nam, Pattaya was the fun place to go. The door-to-door trip from Tan Son Nhat (the Saigon airport) to a beachfront hotel in Pattaya took four hours. A G.I. fighting in the Nam jungles, could get a one-week leave pass at noon, and by evening be sitting in a Pattaya beachfront beer bar with a pretty Thai gal saying, "What would you like me to do for you?"

Pattaya is not located in the Golden Triangle. Rather, it's a twelve-hour drive from Chiang Mai. But, because of its *Anytime is Party Time* atmosphere, the two towns have close opium trade links.

Back in the day,

Chiang Mai was a Wild West town

Before walking outside,

You took a quick look around.

Do you have plans for tonight?

Do you want to come home alive?

Then follow best practice -

Pack a loaded .45

Then our Saigon embassy was overrun

In late April '75.

Our last choppers pulled out,

Our Marines lucky to be alive.

Wild West Atmosphere & Loaded .45's

With the war ended, the US
Could have exited this opium tale,

Except for a Chinese-Shan rebel leader
just released from jail.

He was a ruthless jungle killer.

Khun Sa was his name.

War Lord Extraordinaire

Was the goal of his game.

A Russian doctor hostage swap,
Freed him in Sept '74.

He returned to the poppy fields
Eagerly planning his next score.

War Lord

Extraordinaire

Opium gave Khun Sa the power
And cash he sought.

His one goal – Controlling the heroin;
whether grown, sold or bought.

He knew the trails and hill tribes,
From Yunnan to Chiang Mai.

His troops ruled the jungles.
Small town mayors? Easy to buy.

Want some insights
Into Khun Sa's shtick?

Check out Denzel's
American Gangster flick.

Golden Triangle Map

The Triangle's military and police quickly
got the news.

Money or Death? Khun Sa made deals you
couldn't refuse.

One tale concerned a village chief
Who committed a big No-No.

He sold his town's opium harvest
To Khun Sa's long-time foe.

When Khun Sa arrived,
His army lined up every family in town.

With bullets to the heads, each man,
woman, and child was mowed down.

Shtick – Area of interest or area of activity.

Denzel – The Hollywood film star, Denzel Washington.

American Gangster – A Hollywood film released in 2007 that starred Denzel Washington and Russell Crowe. In the film, Khun Sa was portrayed by the British actor, Ric Young. The film showed Khun Sa's direct connection to the New York City drug trade.

Khun Sa moved his HQ
From Burma to Northern Thailand.

Chiang Mai offered international logistics to
market his brand.

Khun Sa's brother-in-law

Was a high-up in the police.

With payoffs to army generals,

He had security and peace.

During Nam, the US sought partners

To join our quest

For highland fighting in Nam,
The Montagnards were the best.

Nam – Nickname for Vietnam. This nickname was commonly used by G.I.s during the Vietnam War.

Montagnards – A hill tribe in Southeast Asia. The name comes from when the French had control over Vietnam. In French, the word means *Mountain People*. The Montagnards have been put down and persecuted by the Vietnamese for centuries. When the Americans joined the Vietnam War, the Montagnards were viewed as a likely ally. They proved to be an excellent choice. They knew the terrain and they were literally at home living under harsh conditions in the mountains.

Degars – Common French nickname for Montagnards.

Yards – Common American nickname for Montagnards.

They teamed with
US Special Forces early in the war.

Call 'em Yards or Degars,
they rank high in Green Beret lore.

The Vietnamese mocked the Yards
As dumb mountain folks,

Someone to cheat or ridicule
And make the butt of jokes.

But these rugged mountain men
Were brave, fierce and strong

For jungle fighting partners,
The Berets could not go wrong.

Green Berets – The popular name of the American Army Special Forces that was established in 1952. The Special Forces wore Green Berets unofficially and sometimes controversially for several years, until 1961, when President Kennedy authorized the Green Beret to be the official headgear of the Special Forces. Kennedy held the Special Forces in high regard and wanted them to stand out from other military units.

The Green Berets first came to Nam in June 1957 with the responsibility of training indigenous teams to combat the North Vietnamese and the Vietcong. They found the Montagnards to be willing and able warriors who were quite skilled at guerilla warfare. The two organizations formed a close bond that continued beyond the war years.

They'd been downtrodden in Nam
For hundreds of years;

But in their jungle home,
They were bold without fears.

Victims of bigotry gave them

An inborn hatred for the VC;

They'd gladly slit Charlie's throat Before
you count to three.

During peacetime, the Yards were

A typical hill tribe lot,

Self-sufficient subsistence farmers, With
just enough to fill their pot.

Viet Cong – Officially known as the National Liberation Front, the Viet Cong aligned with the North Vietnamese in their fight against the South Vietnamese army and the Americans. Often, the Viet Cong operated as small units of guerilla fighters. Confrontations between Montagnards and the Viet Cong were not uncommon.

The Viet Cong played a major role in the 1968 *Tet Offensive*, one of the major military campaigns in the Vietnam War. During the Tet Offensive, the Viet Cong and North Vietnamese army attacked more than 100 towns and major cities in South Vietnam. The Tet Offensive proved to the world that the opposition to the South Vietnamese government was much greater than the US military leaders had believed.

Where'd they get cash? The poppy
Flowers flourishing in the hills;

The white powder from those poppies
Easily paid the bills.

But, you can't process a harvest,
When fighting in a war.

Meeting their dilemma, Uncle Sam said,
"I'll handle that choir".

The CIA's solution was
Just two countries away.

Khun Sa would handle the process
And with US dollars, gladly pay.

Poppies - Virtually all the hill tribes in Southeast Asia grow opium poppies as a source of revenue. The Montagnards are no exception. Southeast Asia's climate is ideal for growing poppies. The flowers grow in the wild. Their short growing cycle makes them an ideal, profitable cash crop.

CIA – The US Central Intelligence Agency. The CIA gathers foreign intelligence, while the FBI gathers domestic intelligence. The CIA is often criticized for its involvement in sinister, sleazy and questionable activities.

DEA – The US Drug Enforcement Agency.

LZ – The Landing Zone for helicopters.

Chopper – A nickname for a helicopter.

Chinook - A large helicopter that can carry up to three dozen troops and fly more than 180 miles per hour. If there are less than a half dozen troops aboard, the remaining space can be used for cargo.

The problem? Logistics.
Moving the poppies 700 miles.

Nodding at the LZ,
The CIA guy was all smiles --

"1st Cav, I wanna borrow a chopper.
No questions asked.

Give me a Chinook.
They're big and they're fast."

"Get me a fresh crew,
That's all set, and ready to fly.

Their bonus: a night of R'n'R
In old Chiang Mai."

1st Cav - The 1st Cavalry Division or 1st Air Cavalry Division became a major air assault unit during the Vietnam War. The 1st was the first unit to use helicopters on a large scale for virtually every aspect of military involvement. The 1st Cav's insignia. A black horse's head on a yellow shield.

"Tell 'em, in Asia,
Chiang Mai gals are Number One.

It'll be party time, big time
When the job is done."

"My guy will meet your team
When they touch ground.

Within a day or two,
Your guys 'll be homeward bound."

"Khun Sa's the name of the Dude
We're dealin' with.

My guy has set it all up,
No worry. There won't be no shit."

Chiang Mai Gals – Many old Asian hands consider the young women of Chiang Mai to be some of the most beautiful women in Thailand. Coupling this with their small town, country girl charm, many Asian men consider Chiang Mai girls to be ideal wives. Part of their attractiveness is due to their very fair complexions. In Asia, light skin is often viewed as being a very desirable beauty feature. The fair complexions can be traced to the influx of light skinned Burmese people during prior centuries.

Although the author did considerable research on this subject, during his thirty years of living and traveling in Asia, he did not reach any definitive conclusions as to whether Chiang Mai girls are the loveliest in Asia. He feels he would need to do much more research before reaching any clear and definitive conclusions.

"It'll be US cash, up front,
When we make the deal.

My guy'll do the countin'
And make sure the bills are real."

"Khun Sa wants the USA
To be his friend.

The whole thing should go smooth
From beginning to end."

"But remember, you'll be deep inside
Khun Sa's jungle base."

So, best to keep your backup
fully loaded . . . just in case.

Keep your Backup fully loaded

The first shipment went well.
Then, a couple after that.

Everyone was happy.
A Win-Win. Tit for Tat.

Another one of our CIA's
Untold secret wars.

This time, our spooks aided the Yards
In making some big-time scores.

If you can't believe Uncle
Ran a long-term drug deal.

All I can say is, "Come on,
Grow up and get real."

Religion is the opiate of the Masses
- Karl Marx

Opium is the religion of the mountains
- PeriRac

And, also,
Kindly tell me why,

Black Horse Chinooks were seen
Frequenting the Chiang Mai Sky.

The Company does interesting things
To keep bad guys at bay.

Is it red, white and blue?
Or 51 shades of gray.

In April '75, the Nam War ended;
And the U.S. did an about-face;

With big city police chiefs screaming,
"Heroin's flooding the place."

Uncle or Uncle Sam – Nickname for the USA.

Spook – A nickname for a CIA operative.

The Company - A nickname for the CIA.

Manuel Noriega – Panama's dictator from 1983 until 1989. From the 1950's thru the 1980's, Noriega was both, a valued CIA drug informant and a major drug trafficker. The CIA turned a blind eye to this.

In late 1989, Noriega pushed the envelope too far and ticked off Uncle Sam to the max. Shortly thereafter, on December 20, 1989, the USA invaded Panama. Noriega went on the run and took sanctuary in the Vatican Embassy. The USA chose to employ psychological warfare and good old fashion blaring Rock'N'Roll music. I don't know if Noriega was into rock music in his teens, but by his late 50's he could no longer suffer it. On January 3, 1990, Noriega surrendered to U.S. forces. For the next 27 years, until his death in 2017, Noriega remained in prison.

Khun Sa, a helpful friend?
Real fast, that story grew old.

Just like Panama's Noriega,
We threw Khun Sa out of the fold.

After a brief cool silence; Uncle Sam
Reared up his ugly head.

Uncle announced, "We want Khun Sa
D-E-A-D dead.

The U.S. attitude change, didn't sink in with
Khun Sa right away.

First, he was a rejected suitor;
Now, he became Uncle's hunted prey.

We want

Khun Sa

D - E - A - D

Dead

Khun Sa wanted to believe
He was still part of team USA.

"Can't we just go back
To the old way?"

He sent his guys to check.
"Is it true or not?"

They feared to report back.
As bad news messengers often get shot.

The USA then repeated:
"Khun Sa's gotta go down."

When it finally sunk in,
He took it with more than a frown.

Shoot the Messenger

In Bangkok, the capital, the diplomats
All agreed and played nice.

But, up in Chiang Mai,
Everything came with a price.

Chiang Mai, with its tourists, banks
And bars, was a commercial core.

It was also a financial hub;
A great place to make deals and score.

The USA Consulate in Chiang Mai
Had an office for the CIA.

Now, due to opium trade,
It set up another, for the DEA.

American Consulate

The USA needed a no-nonsense guy
To combat the wrong.

They brought in Mike Powers:
Intelligent, tough, and strong.

Just by doing his job, Mike immediately
caused flack.

Khun Sa decided, "Now it's my turn
to push back."

Mike had a wife, Joyce, and
Two toddlers. A true family man.

Khun Sa included this factor
Into his evil revenge plan.

It seems it is not uncommon for our US DEA offices and CIA offices to follow paths that lead to results that are contrary, if not contradictory. Sometimes, one agency chooses to look the other way, when one of its operatives or informants is doing things that are normally considered illegal, such as dealing drugs. Meanwhile, the other agency is trying to halt this activity.

Consequently, we have had various bed partners at various times, who at other times, we choose to lock up. Khun Sa, Noriega, the Montagnards, and the whole Iran-Contra Affair are some examples. One other example in Northern Thailand is the Chinese village of Mae Salong, now known as Santikhiri, near the Burmese border. While the village is remote, it is accessible by automobile. Elements of the KMT, the Chinese nationalist army that was fighting Mao's communist forces, fled there when Mao took power in 1949. That story must wait for another day and another pen.

Mike's family went to the market,
One day just around noon,

They were savagely attacked
By a gun-wielding goon.

The hit man was told he had back-up,
And a getaway car.

But in truth, Khun Sa didn't want
This goon to go anywhere far.

We all know, dead goons
Tell no tales.

In addition, bosses don't want them
To leave any trails.

In general, Thailand criminals are neither confrontational nor aggressive. Normally, behind the back acts of thievery are much more common than crimes of face-to-face robbery. During my time, Thailand and my many visits, I only witnessed a few physical attacks on other persons.

Thailand is known as the Land of Smiles. This is more than just tourist brochure propaganda. It is true. People will always smile at you, no matter what the occasion. Even when someone hates you, he or she will still smile at you.

Just remember, when you go to a Thai bar and a girl smiles at you, it doesn't mean she thinks you are sexy. It simply means she is Thai. Nothing more.

The goon was shocked. His getaway car sped away during the grab.

In panic, he yanked Joyce and one kid Into a small truck's cab.

"The escape car's gone?
That not part of the plan!"

Then six police appeared.
The goon thought, "I'm a dead man."

The family maid had run to Mike's office to get him into the fray.

Mike hurriedly rushed. "Gotta get Joyce and kids out of harm's way."

Chiang Mai Market Area

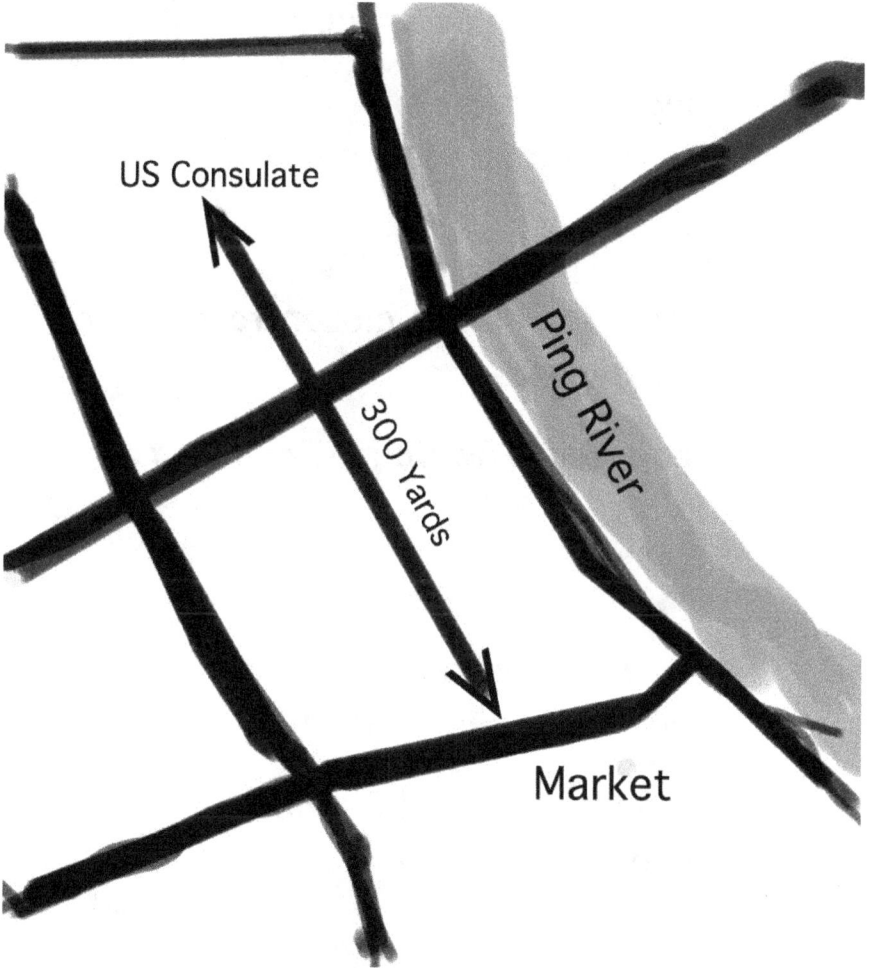

US Consulate

300 Yards

Ping River

Market

Mike stripped to his waist,
Showing no gun or knife.

His negotiation plea:
"Swap me for my son and wife."

Slowly, Mike moved closer to the goon,
Almost eye-to-eye.

He repeated, "Be Calm. Jai Yen Yen,"
Using his best Thai.

He got close enough to take
His child from his wife.

Passing his son to the maid,
Mike returned to save Joyce's life.

Jai Yen Yen! Be calm!

More police arrived
To carry out their part

The goon now knew
He'd been set up from the start.

Khun Sa owned the police,
The goon knew with dread.

The encircling cops had plans
To shoot him dead.

He pressed the gun barrel
Against Joyce's ear.

Her eyes quickly filled
With helpless fear.

Along with the cultural tradition of always maintaining a smile, another Thai trait is negotiation. If you are doing business in Thailand, always be ready for Tit for Tat, and Give and Take negotiation. This is true, even when making a small purchase from a street corner vendor. You will be more readily accepted in Thai society and be much more at ease, when you learn these Thai skills.

When Thais choose not to negotiate, that indicates something is very wrong in the situation. It may well be something you do not understand and it may be in your best interest to back out of the circumstance. The Chiang Mai gunman didn't have a chance to do this. The police had no plans to allow him to back out.

Slowly, Mike walked closer, pondering,
"What can I do?"

Through her tears, Joyce mouthed,
"Honey, I love you."

Then, a loud, Blam!
Joyce's head exploded and shattered.

The windshield turned grey-red.
Blood and brains splattered.

Silence for a moment, then
Mike screamed with deep pain.

Next, police guns roared from all sides.
And the goon was slain.

Joyce Powers
American

Requiescat In Pace
October 1980

Requiescat In Pace – Latin: Rest in Peace.

Now Uncle was truly seething
From Bangkok to D.C.

Its next missive to Thailand –
A no-nonsense decree.

If you want USA aid
To continue to come forth?

Then take immediate action.
Clean up the North.

Bangkok sent Elite Thai Rangers
To resolve the matter.

Their singular order - Bring back
Khun Sa's head on a platter.

Thai Rangers

But this was the North,
And corruption ran deep.

Khun Sa was tipped off
Before the rangers could leap.

While the next ranger attempt
Met with limited success,

Khun Sa learned, if he stayed in Thailand
He'd never get any rest.

And probably, within months,
He'd be gunned down in a fight.

Khun Sa was pragmatic.
"If I wanna live, I gotta take flight."

Fight or Flight

Returning to Burma didn't mean
Khun Sa lost control.

It simply meant he had to add
More middlemen to his dole.

It also meant Burma's Junta
Could force him to play more nice.

And, naturally, the Rangoon generals
Raised their kickback price.

As for me, life in slow Chiang Mai
Made for an easy time.

With that Powers' exception,
There was zilch confrontational crime.

In addition to being totally corrupt, the Burmese Junta is also, totally paranoid and superstitious. Let me correct that. If you think everyone hates you and wants to get rid of you, and it's all true, then you are not paranoid. Correctly, then, the Junta is quite superstitious. In 2005, they feared their own citizens and several foreign elements wanted to overthrow them. What to do? They hurriedly moved the whole government some two hundred miles inland from Rangoon to a farmer's field in the middle of nowhere. This new location, called Naypyidaw, is now the country's capital. Who guided them to do this? A fortuneteller! Yes, a soothsayer who for a fee and favors told them to *Get out of Dodge*. Many civil servants were not informed about the move until 24 hours before it took place. Interestingly, all the foreign embassies chose to stay put in Rangoon and not move to the new location.

Get out of Dodge – American slang that advises people to leave town.

Chiang Mai town is truly
A compact place.

I could walk around it
At a comfortable pace.

Shortly, I found a two-story,
Three-bedroom home,

With a central location,
From which I could easily roam.

My maid oversaw things.
She had a hut out back.

From our many fruit trees,
She'd fix me a daily snack.

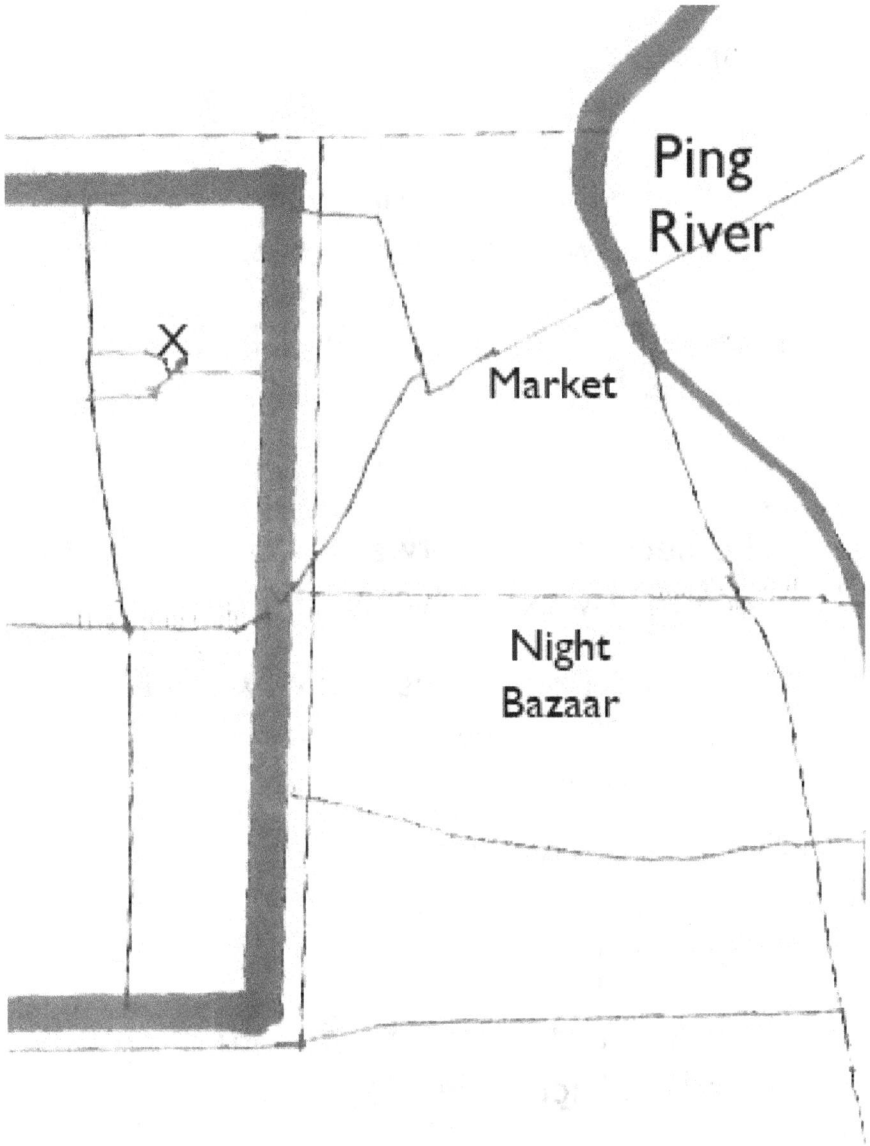

X - The location of the author's old home, just inside the moat at Moon Muang Soi Jet.

I befriended my landlady
And the two men in her life:

The first: a powerful local politician. She
was his Little Wife.

The second: their twenty-year-old son,
Boom. He was both shy and gay.

I noticed Daddy was greatly saddened
By his effeminate way.

The pol's other children
Were from his # 1 wife.

The son: a doctor. The daughter chose
Dad's political life.

In Thailand, a long-term mistress is known as a *Little Wife*. In many Asian countries, *Little Wives* are fairly common among businessmen and government officials. Many businessmen see a *Little Wife* as proof of success. With many poor country girls coming to the city with limited education and job skills, it is not unusual for a businessman to have one or two mistresses. The young lady doesn't have to work. She gets a free apartment, meals and spending money. If he's real busy, she only has to service him a couple times a month.

There is a whole protocol for *Little Wives*. You can take her with you to dinners and evening drinking parties with your close business associates, but you cannot take her to formal meetings with high-ranking government officials. The latter would be too insulting to *Wife # 1*.

In this case, *Wife # 2*, the *Little Wife*, was a college-educated woman and had been with the Pol (Politician) for decades.

They both held deep animosity
For Wife # 2.

Also, as they lived in Bangkok,
Our Meetings were quite few.

Alone in Chiang Mai, Boom seemed lost,
Despite his kind and gentle heart.

Coupled with shy and timid ways,
I couldn't tell if he was smart.

His folks asked me to advise him.
I tried to be his friend.

But a few lunches showed me,
we had no common grounds to blend.

Many young men in Thailand are quite reserved. They tend to be on the shy side and be a bit more gentle and sensitive when compared to western men. This can lead outsiders to believe the guys are gay. While Thailand does have its fair share of gays, you are advised not to make quick judgments. Your personal cultural experiences may be much more limited than you care to admit to yourself.

Many girls find Thai guys to be refreshingly polite when compare to their western counterparts.

His folks appreciated my efforts.
They knew I had tried.

Due to this, and other matters,
They took me on their side.

I even sat in on some stuff
Of the backroom kind.

As I didn't speak much Thai,
No one seemed to mind.

Once they tried smuggling
Two BMWs by raft.

Unfortunately, boating skills
Are not a gangland craft.

Two Beamers Gone in 60 Seconds Flat!

When navigating swift, deep rivers,
Rafts need a balanced load.

Now, the Mae Kong River is
The Beamers permanent abode.

Every three months, I'd do
A Visa Run from Chiang Mai.

The fastest and easiest choice
Was to fly.

I'd just hop a plane
Heading to China's Kunming.

With its ninety-minute flight time,
I kept it a low-key thing.

Beamer – BMW automobile.

Visa Run - Foreigners living outside their home country are commonly referred to as Expats (expatriates). Depending on many factors, Expats can be required to leave the host country at a certain frequency and for a certain amount of time. This is called a Visa Run. In my case, during my Thailand stay, I had to exit the country every 90 days to renew my visa.

Normally, I'd fly to Kunming, China; spend a few days and then return to Chiang Mai. Sometimes, for a change of scenery, I would fly to Singapore or try KL or Penang in Malaysia.

I chose to keep these Visa Runs low key. Only a couple of my friends knew when I left or when I returned. If associates asked where I'd been, I'd just say I'd been sick and resting.

KL – Nickname for Kuala Lumpur.

In the early '90's, Kunming saw
Few Yanks as a rule.

Local college kids liked to hang
With me. It made them feel cool.

I had many party invites
To discos or someone's home.

My hotel rental bicycles,
This made it easy for me to roam.

Once, I arrived just in time
For Stop Drug Trafficking Day.

Five military trucks drove around, Showing
off their display.

Actually, in the past, Kunming was home to a number of Yanks. That was during World War II, when Kunming became the home of the American *Flying Tigers*.

You need to have a little backstory to know the *Flying Tigers*, whose official name was the *1st American Volunteer Group*,

In China, it is difficult to know the backstory, because for more than fifty years, the Communist government has covered up the major role American fighter pilots played in saving China's rear end.

During my visits to Kunming in the early 1990's, I was able to locate a few old timers who told me about the *big and strong* looking Americans on Kunming's streets.

The *Flying Tigers* first aerial combat mission was on December 20, 1941. They brought the fight to the Japanese, while the rest of the US military was still reeling from the shock of Pearl Harbor.

There must have been thirty plus men
Bound up on each truck's flatbed.

The message to all: mess with drugs and
you'll soon be dead.

My friend and I had rented two bikes.
"Let's see where they go."

We had to ride fast if we were going to
catch the rest of the show.

We peddled for 30 minutes.
No time to waste.

Finally, the trucks passed us
And entered a military base.

In six months, the **Flying Tigers** under General Chennault shot down 296 enemy planes and lost only 14 pilots, even though the Japanese planes were faster and much more maneuverable. The yanks used an unorthodox, high altitude **Dive and Zoom** attack plan to beat the enemy. Unfortunately, military bureaucracy, not the Japanese, did them in. They were absorbed into the 14th Air Force.

Eastern China had been under Japanese control before Pearl Harbor. The Chinese forces of Mao and Generalissimo Chiang Kai-shek were too self-absorbed in their own feud to fight the Japanese invaders. China's only supply route in the west: the Burma Road from Rangoon to Kunming.

The **Flying Tigers,** were composed of US Navy, Marine and Army pilots, under a Top Secret Executive Order signed by President F. D. Roosevelt that had them resign from the US military; then volunteer to defend the Burma Road.

The convoy had tinted-windowed Benzes
at the front and rear.

The general's faces were not visible,
Although I was near.

On that narrow road,
When the trucks entered the post,

I could see the convicts' eyes.
They all knew they were toast.

We biked past the compound.
Then climbed up a small hill.

Upon reaching the top,
A thunderous roar gave me a chill.

The *Flying Tigers* made Kunming, China their headquarters just before Pearl Harbor. Japanese pilots quickly learned they'd face extreme prejudice, if they ventured into China's western skies.

The *Flying Tigers* are perhaps best recognized by their nose art.

The *Flying Tigers* were memorialized in the book and the movie, *God is My Co-Pilot.*

The machine guns' rat-a-tat-tat
Overpowered any words I said.

When silence returned, I knew
Those poor souls were all dead.

After the machine gun fire
punctuated the air,

My friend looked at me and said,
"You gotta be fair.

America also has the death penalty.
Isn't that true?"

"Well, even in Texas, we don't do it
Quite like you."

Benz(es) – Nickname for Mercedes Benz.

China is rather secretive about many things including its executions.

There are often told stories that claim when China executes a criminal, it is done with a single bullet to the back of the outlaw's head. Later, after the execution, the government sends a bill to the family of the criminal for the cost of that one bullet. While that story is credible, I can verify, in this instance, I heard machine gun fire, not single shots to the heads. I guess in hindsight it matters little to those one hundred and fifty or more, dead drug dealers who got machine-gunned down.

In touristy Chiang Mai,
Strangers freely talked.

Informal chats were common,
Wherever I walked.

I made many casual friends
While strolling about,

I shortly knew all the cafes and bars
Inside and out.

The hill tribe peoples
I did not yet know.

The tribes had names like
Lisu, Akha, Lahu, and Meo.

Major Hill Tribes in Thailand

Lisu

Ahka

Lahu

Meo

Yao

Karen

Hmong

Palaung

I'd see their young women
Selling goods on the street.

But other than a smile and "Hello,"
We never did meet.

In Thai society, the hill tribes
Didn't quite fit,

They stayed to themselves,
And remained close knit.

My language skills being Zero,
I couldn't stop and chat.

During the first few months
I just left it at that.

For many years, the Thai government and Thai society ignored and mistreated the hill tribe peoples. Then, a few years after World War II ended, many western societies began to prosper. Around that time, air travel became more affordable and popular. The more affluent westerners got off their feet, and sat down on airline seats in order to fly to Asia and other distant places.

Also, in 1949, the Thailand government formed the Tourism Authority of Thailand, known as TAT. Within a short time, TAT came to a certain realization and chose to paraphrase Mark Twain – "There's Gold in them thar hill tribes."

Camera totting tourists pay money to see people and things that are different. The hill tribes of Northern Thailand fit this bill. Alas, the Thai government realized by spending a few dollars on simple water lines to the villages, hundreds of tourist dollars would pour into the Thai economy. It worked.

The young women dressed
In their tribe's styles.

They negotiated with calculators
And shy, beguiling smiles.

Bargaining with them
Was sorta fun and kinda nice.

But their English was limited to,
"I give you best price."

To really know the Triangle,
You must bond with a hill tribe.

You can't do it, by short tourist treks Or
an under-table bribe.

I Give You

Best Price

I'd befriended a few hill tribe members,
who lived in Chiang Mai,

But they, after a few years in town,
Were outsiders, just as much as I.

After some time, I became friends
With two Benelux guys.

They'd been in the North for a while
And had hill tribe ties.

They were both dopers,
Sallow-eyed, more gaunt than slim.

The Dutch guy was Gerald.
The Belgian was Ahka Jim.

Benelux – The area of Europe that consists of three countries – Belgium, the Netherlands and Luxembourg. The three countries are often linked together because they are quite a bit smaller than their neighbors - France, Germany and Italy.

Doper – Someone who does drugs.

Sallow-eyed and gaunt – This can be a sign that a person is a drug addict.

Ahka – One of the hill tribes. Jim had learned the Ahka language well enough to converse fluently. He could also manage to communicate in several other Triangle languages.

Jim could meld with the tribes
Thanks to his linguistic skills.

Much of the time, he just drifted
Through the hills.

He'd mastered border crossings
In the darkness of night.

And clandestinely, he'd cross Burma
And China when in flight.

He told me, when moving China White
Got too hot,

Lijiang, with its Naxi women,
Was his go-to spot.

Ahka Jim

His occupational hazard –
Local police making a fuss,

But the pleasurable Naxi gals
Made his getaways a plus.

Whenever he drifted into town,
He kept his profile low.

What he did? Who he saw?
Local police always wanted to know.

He'd leave a coded mark on my gate,
When in town on the sly.

Usually, we'd meet in a bar
On the outskirts of Chiang Mai.

Lijiang – A city in the northwest part of China's Yunnan Province. Lijiang is a picturesque town of waterways and bridges. Its fame goes back to the ancient southern Silk Road when it was a major trade center silk embroidery center. Now, it has become a popular destination for college students on Spring Break. Unfortunately, in recent years, it has also been discovered by package tours from China's growing middle class who come in large tour buses and create Disneyland-like lines at the more scenic spots.

Naxi – The Naxi minority were the majority in the Lijiang area. Naxi (modern writers call them Nakhi or Nashi), are tied to the Mosuo people and are viewed as a matriarchal society. Without getting into a sociological debate, Naxi women have ruled the roost, handled the money and were the main income earners. They view men, perhaps quite accurately, as irresponsible louts and drunkards who are dependable for sex and little else.

Doing drugs in the Triangle
Is not a big thing.

Smuggling 'em out?
Now, that's a different song to sing.

Too many pros
Have their vested claims.

They'll smash down any attempts
To cut into their games.

In the Triangle, police and army
Definitely held sway,

They controlled most drug trade,
Both night and day.

Police and Army Shootouts

In Thailand, it is not uncommon to hear stories about members of the Thai police getting into a shootout with member of the Thai army.

Backstory – Each of Thailand's seventy-six provinces has some sort of military presence. In those towns where there is a military installation, the young soldiers unsurprisingly frequent the bars, gambling places and house of prostitution.

Normally, the police oversee these places and get certain gratuities for the so-called protection they provide. In Army towns, the local military commander logically argues, these are my guys so I should get a piece of the action. If a suitable split is not arranged, arguments and gunfights can and do erupt.

For those Farangs,
Who were tempted to deal,

There's 10 years in Bang Kwang
To curb their zeal.

If you're new to Thailand,
There's two places you should know.

The first is, Bangkok's Khao San Road,
Where low-end backpackers go.

On Khao San, you'll find
Many types of people from afar,

You may get the feeling
You're in a Star Wars bar.

Farang – A foreigner. Farangs, normally, are foreigners from western countries. Most of the westerners visiting Thailand are Europeans or Australians, rather than Americans. Thailand is tourist friendly and the closest Asian country to Europe.

Khao San Road – An area of cheap hotels and backpacker lodgings near the old downtown area of Bangkok. Khao San Road has its own regular hourly bus from the airport. Any travel book that features ***Bangkok on Ten Dollars a Day*** features Khao San Road. Its cafes are casual and laidback. Backpackers feel quite free to chat with whoever is at the next table.

Bang Kwang – The notorious Bangkok prison where most foreigners end up after being arrested for smuggling or selling drugs. During the Olympics or the World Cup Games, Bang Kwang has enough foreigners from the major countries to form its own football (***soccer*** for American readers) tournament.

The second is Bang Kwang prison,
A real terrible place.

Bang Kwang also houses people
Of every race.

Dreams of quick money
and being cool, you see,

Can turn a young traveler
Into a smuggling wannabe.

Gerald chose a different path:
Life in a Black Lahu baan.

He became a farmer.
He felt this had no real con.

Wannabe – Slang for someone who dreams of being someone else, such as a wannabe movie star.

Baan – In general, a baan is a small village. Hill tribe baans are often scattered in rather remote locations.

Mason Jar – A glass jar used for home canning and for preserving food. John Mason invented Mason jars in 1858. In the old days, when there were many small family farms and many people grew their own vegetables and fruits, Mason jars were quite common. They are still in use today, to a much lesser degree, with the Ball brand being the most popular ones.

.

To ease his load, he took
A 14-year-old wife.

He then settled into
A simple hill tribe style life.

Gerald grew vegetables
And helped his wife's dad.

He also grew opium.
Yeah, his cash flow wasn't bad.

He'd motorcycle into town,
And sell his stuff in bars.

Small plastic bags were
Gerald's version of Mason Jars.

Gerald
The Farmer

Different cultures moralize
On what is right and wrong.

Some pray to rain gods.
Some sing a hymnal song.

Each has unique traditions
And centuries-old ways

Their people have passed these down
Since olden days.

If you're unfamiliar
With the Lahu tribal scene,

Many Lahu gals wed
When they turn fourteen.

A 14 Year Old Wife

They marry Lahu boys,
Who move in with her clan,

The boy joins her family
And works for her old man.

This arrangement goes on
For a year or two.

Drug addiction causes
Most marriages to fall through.

When they break up,
She looks to marry again.

Her dad is philosophical,
"WTF. A new hired hand."

Joint United Nations and World Health Organization study.

A joint United Nations and World Health Organization study found a high level of opium addiction among the various hill tribes of Thailand. The young male addicts were found to use 3.9 grams of opium per day and had been using opium on average for approximately eight years.

From my personal experience, I believe this study is highly accurate.

WTF – What The F*ck

Hitching up with a foreigner
Is a true rarity at best.

Her dad eagerly seeks a dowry:
"How about two grand...US?"

If the marriage is short-lived,
Her dad doesn't pout.

For sure, he's already blown the cash; On
that there is no doubt.

Gerald had been married four years
When I met Na, his wife.

With their young daughter,
They lived a simple, happy life.

The Thai government seems to view hill tribe people as outsiders. Living in remote areas, the hill tribe people move freely across open jungle and forest borders. They do not use hospitals; midwives deliver babies; and, they do not attend Thai schools. There are no birth certificates nor school records. As a matter of fact, there are no records of any kind showing proof that they are residents of Thailand. Consequently, it is nearly impossible for any of them to get a Thai passport. So, this makes it virtually impossible for them to travel or migrate to Europe, Australia or the USA.

Gerald encouraged my visits,
Welcoming me with warm cheers.

Then we'd sit up half the night,
Chatting over warm beers.

My first visit, I crashed
At Na's brother's place.

I slept on the floor.
There was barely enough space.

The guy was totally zonked,
24-7, every day.

He was hardly aware of me
during my short stay.

Sleeping in the hut of a doper wasn't too bad. He left me alone and I showed him the same respect. As a matter of fact, he hardly moved. Most of the time, he sat in a cross-legged position, just looking blankly at the space in front of him. If he would have fallen over dead, I would not have been surprised.

The hut was quite small, maybe twelve foot by twelve foot. It was not a place to hang out during day light hours. At night, in total darkness, I'd enter the hut with my flashlight and find my little sleeping mat. Within minutes, I'd be asleep. I'd awaken around sunrise and leave. Occasionally, I took an afternoon nap. The few times I saw my housemate, he was in a drug stupor and seemed not to notice me.

During that visit,
I enjoyed the village scene,

Observing the locals
In their daily routine.

Pretty much, I just relaxed
And sorta just chilled out,

I shot a lot of pictures
And just wandered about.

In opium land, a new face
Gets a suspicious eye.

But as "Gerald's Best Friend,"
I was now a Made Guy.

A
Made
Guy

A Made Guy – From gangster slang. It means someone they can trust.

The more we sat around
Drinking warm beer,

The more the villagers knew
I was no one to fear.

Occasionally, trekkers
Passed through this way.

A Lahu host can earn ten bucks
For a night's stay.

Gerald told me of an incident
From a few months before,

Concerning a trekker's new boots
Left outside a hut's door.

Trekker – Normally, the trekkers were western backpackers who were hiking around through the hills and exploring the Golden Triangle on their own.

Farang - A commonly used term for a foreigner. While its origin is argued, it seems to be tied to the name the Thais used for French people when the French had a major role in Southeast Asia. Now, Farang refers to any Caucasian foreigner. The word Farang doesn't by itself connote anything negative.

It seems wherever I go I get a nickname. In Hawaii, I am called a Haole; in the city of Guangzhou in southern China, I am called a Gweilo; in Northern China, I am a Laowai, and in Japan, a Gaijin. My attitude about it: Whatever!

Baht - The baht is the basic currency of Thailand. Currently, 35 baht equal a dollar. When I lived in Chang Mai it was 40 to the dollar.

Overnight, the boots disappeared.
His host felt deep shame.

He pled to all, "It musta been
A mistake. No one's to blame.

The Farang is leaving soon.
He needs his boots back.

No need to explain.
Just return them outside my shack."

Shortly, the Farang departed,
Wearing makeshift flip-flops.

With no one coming forward,
Discussion of the matter stops.

These boots were made for walkin'

Two days later, the host, with boots
In hand, hurried to town.

He said he found them and wanted
To track the Farang down.

Claiming success, the host returned
Within a few days.

And the baan seemed to go back
To its normal ways.

Then, a week later, a healthy neighbor
Was found dead in his pad.

All covered in vomit & diarrhea.
Wolfsbane poisoning! A very nasty bad.

Wolfsbane - Also known as Monkshood or Devil's Helmet is a truly toxic flowering plant that grows in mountainous areas.

Don't let the beauty of the plant fool you. It is extremely toxic. The Chinese have used it when hunting large animals and in battle, they would put it on the tips of arrows. Wolfsbane can start affecting the body within twenty minutes after contact.

Chinese herbal medicine practitioners use Wolfsbane in exceedingly limited amounts, to relieve pain. If you use too much, you will never, ever feel pain again.

Baht Buses - Pickup trucks that are converted into shuttle bus taxies. They are very common and convenient in the Chiang Mai area. Some roam around town, others have fixed routes to nearby towns. Their cargo areas have roofs and two long wooden benches inside. Riders hop on and off whenever and wherever they wish.

To get up to the hills,
I depended on my motorbike.

My first stop, the Baht Bus station
To sort of hitchhike.

I would cut a deal with a driver,
And throw my bike on top.

Some 90 klicks up Hwy 118,
I'd signal where to stop.

Next, it's a bumpy trail ride,
For seven more klicks.

Yeah, Black Lahu baans
Are truly in the sticks.

Normally, baht buses charge low, flat fixed rates that depend upon the destination. In town, I would pay around 5 baht for a baht bus ride. Quite cheap.

By comparison, Tuk-Tuk's, the three-wheeled taxies, often try to charge Farangs from US$5 to US$10 for a one-mile ride. Tuk-Tuk's are open aired, but have roofs.

When going to the hills, I'd motorbike to the bus station and look for buses heading to Chiang Rai. I'd tell the driver where I wanted to hop off and agree to pay extra for putting my motorbike on the roof. Other riders would get off before or after me. When we neared my destination, I'd tap on the window that separated the driver's cab from the passengers. The driver would stop the bus; I'd pay him and get my bike off the roof. Then we parted. He continued to Chiang Rai and I drove five klicks on the winding mountain path to the baan.

The small huts are
Made of bamboo and wood.

They're almost satisfactory.
It's a stretch to say they're good.

The baan's forty or so huts
Seemed to be 40 shades of brown.

Some were built on stilts,
A meter above the ground.

Others were linked together
And made into one,

Normally, for a married daughter,
sometimes for a son.

The huts are small and basic, with just one or two rooms. They do not have electricity and are dark inside. They get natural sunlight by leaving the front door open.

The cooking is done inside the hut; normally in a big pot in the center of the main room. There is no chimney. The smoke turns into soot on the ceiling.

The walls of the huts are made from pieces of wood that are loosely fit and not sealed. This allows air in and out. At first, I viewed this as poor workmanship, but because the Lahu cook inside their homes. The holes allow the cooking and heating smoke to exit the hut. In general, I did not consider the huts to be healthy places to reside for more than one or two weeks at a time.

A water supply is valuable
In any remote scene.

This baan had a water line, so that
all could cook and clean.

With the baan's dusty circumstance
And hot noonday sun,

A cool, refreshing shower
Was a relief for everyone.

While traditional Lahu clothing
Is rather chaste,

At the baan's public shower,
All went nude above the waist.

Everyone Nude Above the Waist

The shower was
The village gossip spot.

There, friends talked privately,
Out of other's earshot.

Also, each Lahu baan
Has a circular corral with a gate.

It's used for traditional dancing
During every special fete.

On Lunar New Year, the gals danced
Late into the night.

They used a couple generators
To provide adequate light.

In my experiences, traditional Lahu folk dancing is perhaps best compared to American barn dancing or round dancing. Pretty much, it is mainly the young ladies who participate. However, there is a leader, with a large mouth gourd instrument who sets the beat and pipes out the music. The gals line up shoulder-to-shoulder with perhaps two to four young ladies abreast. While guys can join in, it seemed the guys just sit around getting stoned.

The music and dancing go on for hours, with the music becoming somewhat hypnotic as the evening draws on. I don't know how late, because I got tired of watching and went back to my hut and fell asleep. In the total darkness of the hills, it is easy to fall asleep, especially if you've had more than a few shots of straight SangSom rum.

A few klicks from this baan
Was a backpacker hideaway.

A Druggie Lodge where wannabe dopers
could get high every day.

There, trekkers could try smack
Or whatever they please,

Without the ugly urban experience
Of dirty backroom sleaze.

Upon returning to Chiang Mai,
I read up on Lahu cultural ways.

And made plans to return
At Lunar New Year; all fourteen days.

Klick – *Klick* is slang for kilometer. The term is commonly used in rural areas in those countries that use meters for measurement. It is commonly used in Thailand.

A Buck – One dollar.

White Lightning – A high alcohol whiskey. Every country has one. Normally, farmers using rice, wheat or sugar cane created them centuries ago. In China, it is baijiu and the popular brand is Maotai. In Thailand, the white (or brown) lightening is called whiskey, but is more closely kin to rum. Two popular brands are SangSom and Mekhong.

Ganbei – A Chinese toast meaning empty your glass, or bottoms up.

For this visit, everyone accepted me.
I was Gerald's old friend.

This made it much easier for me
To interact and blend.

Gerald got me a private hut.
I paid US 5 bucks a night.

The owner - an old widow,
Suffering financial plight.

I ate with her family. We sat in
a circle, around a big stew pot.

They had a fire underneath
To keep the soupy food hot.

While my home in Chiang Mai was quite large and had a kitchen and all the normal kitchen appliances, I ate virtually all my meals in restaurants. The restaurant meals and drinks were quite cheap; and I enjoyed roaming around town and socializing.

For exercise, I used an upscale health club and swimming pool. For entertainment, there were many restaurants and bars. Many of the bars had live music. My social life was quite active.

This made my maid's life easy. She didn't have to cook for me. She watched several Thai soap operas every day. She had a three-room hut on the property. She acted as my home's security guard and insured no one would sneak in when I was out.

There were five types of fruit trees on the premise. My maid normally prepared a bowl of fresh fruit for me after my afternoon nap.

The old widow chomped down food
With a toothless mouth.

At every meal, this alone
Tended to gross me out.

Our stew was dished up
From a central pot.

Not too sanitary. But in the hills, That's all
you got.

If someone didn't finish
Their bowl of stew,

The leftovers were thrown back
For tomorrow's brew.

One of my friends in Chiang Mai was a Red Lahu gal who was a student at Chiang Mai University. She did not wear Lahu clothing and had left her baan as a young teen. She no longer had close ties to her old lifestyle. She told me she felt somewhat like a lost soul, as she lived on the edges of the Red Lahu, Thai and Farang cultures without belonging to any of them.

Perhaps, because of this, she chose to write her term paper for English class on the fourteen days of the Red Lahu Lunar New Year Festival. On each day, certain traditions were followed and she wanted to explain this in detail in her writings. She didn't own a computer and her written English skills were marginal. She asked if she could use my computer and asked if I would review and critique her term paper.

This paper piqued my interest in the Lahu New Year celebration. Later, when Gerald suggested I spend the Lunar New Year in his baan, I said, "Why not?"

I brought lemon juice vials
To this challenging scene,

With hopes these would kill bacteria and
keep my food clean.

One night a translator
Was invited to join our evening meal.

The widow's teen daughter-in-law Brought
him, to offer me a deal.

She wanted to dump her druggie Husband
and come live with me.

With both parents dead, she was
A bargain. There was no dowry.

Throughout my whole life, I have been unskilled when it comes to learning languages other than English. I suppose, now that I am over seventy-five, I guess I never will. I have taken formal classes in six different languages and have pretty much failed miserably at all of them. I have learned to APL when needing a translator.

When traveling in other countries, I try to learn a few key phrases: "I want a beer." "How much does it cost?" And "I think you're very beautiful." I've learned these few short phrases can take you very far.

Another travel tip: Always APL (Ask a Pretty Lady). When you need information, pull out the map. (Always carry a map, even when one's not needed. You want to look like a lost tourist.) Look for a nicely dressed gal who appears college educated. (All college students learn some English.) On a city street corner, a gal is more likely to help a lost tourist, than talk to a strange guy who appears to be trying to hustle her.

I thought, "Gal, don't talk that way
In front of your husband's clan.

You're gonna make him lose face
And be a lesser man."

Any way you look at it, I thought,
This gal just ain't cool.

She surely never learned the basics
In Mrs. Potter's etiquette school.

I told her she seemed
quite lovely and nice.

But for me, marriage,
just wasn't in the dice.

While I lack language skills, I can eat and drink just about anything and everything. This ability has allowed me entry to many situations and acceptance in many cultures.

During my travels in remotes spots, I don't wince when my host serves dog, cat, rat, lizard or other strange delicacies.

I've eaten many types of snakes including the poisonous ones the waiter brings to the table alive. In these instances, the waiter holds the two-foot long serpent by its tail and lets it move a bit to show it still has fight.

The waiter then cuts the snake down its length with a razor and allows the blood and gallbladder to drip into the canister of white lightening. He then says "Enjoy!" as we chug-a-lug and he before preparing the rest of the snake for dinner.

Quickly I invented
A Chiang Mai girlfriend/wife.

Then I explained
How I traveled most of my life.

Later, I wondered, "My hut?
Am I renting the couple's old shack?"

"Maybe, he took off,
And isn't coming back."

Whatever. I figured it best
To stay away from this young lass.

If she'd make another offer,
I'd be curt. "No thanks. I pass."

This dinning ability has allowed me to meld with the locals in many places. In Guangzhou, where I lived for ten years, the dining guideline is, "If it has four legs and it's not the table, you eat it." I fit in well.

This ability has gained me an invite to a dinner and sleepover at Kazak horseman's family yurt in the Xinjiang Mountains. On another occasion, it took me on an oxcart ride to a home-cooked meal at a Hmong village outside Kunming. One secret: In remote places always carry a small plastic squeeze bottle of ReaLemon concentrate. It kills bacteria quickly.

During our most recent visit, a dozen Chinese Electronic Surveillance Police (old friends) hosted my wife and I in a small-town hotel. After too much **Ganbei** toasting, the Chinese government kindly comped our hotel bill. Another travel secret: I claim the only alcohol my religion allows is beer. By saying this, I avoid toasting with the more potent baijiu.

Gerald and I were chatting
On the third day.

His wife came up shyly,
With something to say.

She smiled and looked into my eyes
With excited, innocent glee.

"Can you, er, will you,
Take a shower with me?"

Caught off guard, I looked at Gerald
With a shocked fluster.

Then I quickly stammered,
"Gerald, I've never touched her."

will you
take a shower
with me?

He laughed at my embarrassment,
"No need to fear.

She wants you to live in the baan,
And feel welcome here."

Then she led me to the shower.
We both stripped to our waists.

I was shy to look at her.
She, giggling, splashed water in my face.

Then, four of her friends ran up,
Stripped down, and joined the fun.

They all liked the splash game.
It was five against one.

Five against One

The girls were emboldened.
I was Gerald's best friend and guest.

Na had Gerald's blessing. They,
As her friends, could join in the jest.

The next day, Na and her water sprite
Posse knocked at my door.

I hurried to consult Gerald,
"Again? And how many times more?"

His wife had told him, one or two gals
Had a shine for me.

And "Their dads are well aware you
can pay a high dowry fee."

One thing to learns about Southeast Asia, many relationships are related to money. Often, this is due to the income disparity. Why are the young ladies from the countryside attracted to traveling western guys? Trust me, in the clear majority of instances, it's about money. We western guys want to believe we are so cool and debonair. Maybe, we are, to a point, but then, the money factor kicks in and carries the ball over the goal line.

One Thai wife in Munich told me her story. When she was fifteen she left her village to look for a job in Pattaya. She knew her former neighbor was working as a waitress in a restaurant. She hoped her friend could help her find a job. When she arrived, she found her friend was a barmaid in a side street strip joint. Her friend was talking with a customer. She said she was leaving with the customer for an **all-nighter** and would not be back until 10:00 the next morning.

"Gerald, you know I don't want
Any kind of wife.

And a teenage Lahu gal
Won't fit in with my rambling life."

Gerald laughingly smiled and suggested
I just play along.

"Otherwise you'll offend their families.
Just don't do any wrong."

He gave me more advice to maneuver
This slippery ditch.

"Just look, but Don't Touch,
If you don't want to hitch."

Her friend and the tourist left. My friend was alone, with just a few bucks in her purse. While contemplating what to do, an Aussie sat down and offered to buy her a drink. As she had not eaten, he also bought her lunch. They talked. He took her to his room and they had sex. It was her first time. They stay together another night and he gave her US $20. She couldn't believe a man could love her that much. She was totally in love. Then, after breakfast, he told her she was nice, but he was in town for only a week and wanted to try one or two more gals before returning to Sydney.

Dumbfounded, shocked and confused, she returned to the bar. Her old girlfriend introduced her to the Mama-San who offered her a job. That night she became one more Pattaya bargirl, pulling **short-timers** and/or **all-nighters**. Six months later, a German guy showed up and offered to marry her. Now, she's a hausfrau, a housewife, in Munich. She's not really happy, but it's better than being a Pattaya bargirl.

He promised, after a few days,
He'd talk with his wife.

"In the meantime, Enjoy!
There are worse things in life."

So, Na called upon her husband's
"Best friend" several times each day.

She brought along her teenage posse,
To smile, shower, and play.

It was fun, but one night, I was awoken
by footsteps under my shack.

My half-awake thought,
"There's a gang. I'm under attack."

In the bars of Bangkok, Pattaya, Phuket and Chiang Mai it is pretty much the same. If the barmaid chooses to go with a customer, the customer must pay a bar fine to the Mama-Sa. Back then, the bar fine was US $5.00. The bar gets its money up front. After that, what happens and the amount of money paid are negotiation points between the customer and barmaid

Usually, the first factor is how long the gal will stay with the guy. An **all-nighter** means she'll stay until breakfast. A **short-timer** means she'll stay around two hours or just long enough to earn her pay.

In Bangkok, if the guy asks her to stay for a few nights, they must decide upon what to do during the daytime. The girl says she has seen all the tourist sights, but she has an idea. "Let's go to the new shopping center! I'll show you the jewelry and fashion departments, and you can show me just how much you love me."

Stilt legs held my hut up,
A meter above the ground.

Were there three or four guys
Below me, slowly moving around?

Was it a jealous lover,
Who wanted to see me die?

Had he brought some friends
To ensure my permanent goodbye?

Also, in this hilly region,
Drug smuggler groups held sway.

Had I overstayed my welcome?
Was I was getting in their way?

When you walk through the shopping malls of Bangkok, don't be surprised to see attractive young Thai gals dressed in cocktail dresses being followed by unshaven Farangs who are dressed in T-shirts, beach shorts and flip flops.

If you are a male Farang and are arriving in Bangkok for the first time, there is one thing you should know. If you want to date nice Thai women, you must always dress nice. Wear long pants and a clean shirt with a collar. If you look like a beach tourist, the Thais you pass on the street will presume the gal you are with is a bargirl. No girl wants her neighbors to think she works in a Thai tourist bar.

They'd boldly killed a DEA agent's wife
In the center of town.

In these remote hills,
It'd be easy to take me down.

I could be knifed or speared from below
While lying on my mat.

If some thrusts came upward,
I'd be dead in seconds flat.

Many thoughts bounced in my brain.
I was now fully awake.

I knew I had just a few moments,
If I were to make my break

I figured my best chance for survival
Was to stand and fight.

I prepared for a final confrontation
On that black, starless night.

My only weapon
Was a simple flashlight.

I decided not to turn it on
Until I jumped into the fight.

I moved quickly, and leaped
From the door to the ground.

Doing a full 360, I surveyed
Everything as I spun around.

A Fight til Death?

What I saw, caught me by surprise
And made me freeze.

Confused and bewildered,
I fell to my knees.

It took a few moments
To focus my eyes.

And see there were no killers
Nor any kind of bad guys.

My flashlight brightened the ground
Under my hut.
It showed a scene that was
all butt and gut.

When the sun goes down in the Golden Triangle, it is totally dark. The few campfires go out a few hours after sunset. After that, total darkness. Total darkness for miles and miles and miles in all directions. Only when there is a full moon is there any visibility.

It is easy to understand how past generations have had tales of ghosts and other world creatures. Lying on the floor of a hut, in total darkness, it is easy to get spooked; especially if there is any kind of wind.

Rather than crazed killers,
There were five large pigs

Chomping and nibbling
On weeds and twigs.

I felt rather embarrassed
as I chuckled at my plight

But was truly quite relieved
I didn't have to fight.

I went back to sleep knowing
I wasn't going to die.

In the morn, I decided, "Maybe,
it's time to return to Chiang Mai."

Piper and Black Lahu dancers.

Lunar New Year had ended, so
I headed to Chiang Mai town.

Due to my loss of appetite, my waistline
had slimmed down.

While I never chose a Lahu bride
Or even a live-in queen,

Thanks to my frequent showers,
I Stayed very, very clean.

I wondered, "For Lahu gals,
Do looks or money matter?"

After glancing in my mirror,
I conceded, alas, it was the latter.

In Chiang Mai, I had a rather active social life. I had taken early retirement. I retired at age 51, in Munich, Germany. When I rented my home in Chiang Mai, I was 52.

I had three Thai lady friends whom I saw at least once a week. All three owned their own automobiles, so economically, they were several cuts above the average Chiang Mai gal. Two of the ladies had university degrees.

The first was simply a good friend. We were not involved romantically. She was an accountant in her mid-twenties. I could depend upon her to pick me up at the airport when I arrived and see me off when I departed on one of my many trips. She also helped me when I needed a Thai perspective or something official, such as a driver's license. I saw her, maybe once a week. She wanted to learn about the west; I wanted insights into Thai mindsets.

In reflection, I don't believe
I broke any young lady's heart.

But maybe some fathers' pocketbooks
Were sad to see me part.

Three months later, I returned to Munich
for an extended stay.

After that, it was six months
of travel and study, in the good old USA.

Because of my travels,
It was more than a year

Before I could return
to the land of Singha beer.

The second gal was a clothing designer who owned a dress shop that catered to tourists. She was in her early thirties, kind and exceedingly shy. I had trouble with her shyness, but she was a dependable friend. Sometimes, we took weekend holidays using her automobile.

The third Thai lady was a high-ranking government official, who had transferred up from Bangkok. She was 40-something; definitely, upper class; always impeccably dressed; and always looked as if she had just stepped out of a fashion magazine.

Once, we bumped into a German friend and his Thai wife. Later, my friend's wife told me, she never thought a Thai woman of that high social status would date a Farang.

I had met the government official, while buying a train ticket. We hit it off and soon were dating several times a week. Our dates often started at a health club or swimming pool, right after work.

First, one night in Bangkok,
then to the north I did fly

To my former hometown,
scenic old Chiang Mai.

First, I checked into a hotel
and rented a motorbike.

Then I checked out
the various bars I used to like.

In the morning, I rode out
To my former landlady's place.

Though very happy to see me,
Sadness covered her face.

Our dating routine had one peculiarity. We only dated from Monday to Thursday. Every Friday morning, she took the train to Bangkok and every Monday afternoon, she returned to Chiang Mai via train.

She had two rules. Other than those two rules, we had a very close relationship that could have gone further. Rule One concerned her personal life: "Ask me no questions and I will tell you no lies."

Rule Two was also simple. If I happened to be in Bangkok on a weekend, I should never, even think about contacting her. I could handle both these rules as this freed me up on the weekends, to do my thing; date other Thai gals; or hook up with Asian and Western tourists. As for Bangkok, no problem. I had several friends there, and if there's any place in the world to have a boy's night out, Bangkok's that place.

The only personal thing she shared: Her brother was an admiral in the Thai navy.

Her eyes were filled with tears.
She Looked aged and pale.

After her maid served us tea,
She unloaded her tale.

Her circumstances had changed
More than a lot.

Listening, I wondered, "Am I
One of the few friends she's got?"

Her husband and her son were gone.
Both were dead.

Now her life, a void, overshadowed
By constant dread.

In Thailand, virtually everyone has a nickname that their mother gave them right after birth. Three common nicknames Lek, Nit, and Noi all mean "small" or "tiny." Pui means, "chubby" or "plump." It is a bit comical to call a ninety-pound, thirty-year-old woman, Plump. Also, Thai women in general are quite comfortable going through life with "Chubby" as their nickname.

One of the realities of Thailand: Thai family names are unbelievably long. They normally have a minimum of twelve letters. I really appreciated the fact that they use nicknames. The down side, many gals have the same nickname. When I answered the phone and the gal says, "Hi, this is Lek." I had to try to figure out which Lek it is.

Her politician husband had died
Nine months before.

His false friends no longer came
To call at their door.

"The Strong Man of the North"
Was killed by a diseased liver.

As her story continued,
Her body started to quiver.

Boom had been murdered
Three months after that.

Payback to the Little Wife?
Revenge? A belated tit for tat?

Getting around Chiang Mai can be a bit awkward if one doesn't have his own set of wheels. Initially, I walked everywhere. As I have run more than a few marathons, I never really mind walking a mile or two. However, as the daily Fahrenheit temperature in Chiang Mai is regularly in the nineties, I knew I was going to sweat a lot. Also, the main streets are always congested with traffic, noise and pollution. This makes it generally unpleasant to walk around town.

The baht buses are an economical way to hop around the city. Normally, I took my motorbike or a baht bus, when I went shopping; visited a doctor or went to other places that were not part of my daily routine.

Boom had gone bike riding,
As he did every afternoon;

He followed a twenty-klick loop
To keep his body in tune.

By dinner that evening,
Boom had failed to return.

She then drove his bike route,
Out of fear and concern.

She found his bike and backpack
Near a drainage stream.

Later, she realized how this location
fit into the scheme.

After a few months, I bought a second-hand motorbike for a few hundred dollars. This gave me greater freedom, especially in the evenings. None of my three lady friends would ride on the back of my motorbike. That was fine. We would use their cars and they would drive me around town.

Before I got the motorbike, the Tuk-Tuks would continually bother me. A Tuk-Tuk is an open cab, auto rickshaw. Tuk-Tuk drivers would continually stop me and ask, "Where you going?" Then, presuming I was a tourist, would try to grossly over charge me. US$10 for a ride that should cost US$.50. That gets old quickly, especially if it happens every time you walk down the street.

By the way, "Where you going?" is a common Thai countryside salutation. It seems to come from the small village society, when a villager saw a friend walking out of town, he was probably going somewhere he normally didn't go.

After another two days,
She discovered Boom's fate.

His body was found downstream,
Stuck in a watershed gate.

She handed me photos
Showing his head severely bashed.

He'd suffered a serious clubbing
Before his body was trashed.

The police investigation
Was quick and short:

"We found a beer can.
He got drunk and fell in." End of report.

After buying a motorbike, the Tuk-Tuk annoyance went away. The new annoyance was the crazy, erratic drivers. But hey, life is an adventure. I was reminded of this often, especially at night, when I saw motorbike drivers crash into cars and sometimes quite literally bite the dust. Normally, I chose not to drive my motorbike at night. Too dangerous.

A second annoyance related to the fact that I had bought a second-hand motorbike. It worked fine. No problems. Most of the time, my driving distance was short – a mile or two. The annoyance was from gas station attendants and other motorbike drivers who told me as a (presumably rich) Farang, I should be driving a newer and more stylish motorbike.

I was very aware of the black market for stolen motorbikes. When I parked my old beat-up bike to have lunch, I felt very comfortable knowing no one would choose to steal it.

In the North, when the rich
And powerful have special needs,

They often call their police connections
to do their dirty deeds.

Her rental properties were seized.
She knew there's little she could do.

"Your son had misfortune.
Don't let the same happen to you."

When I rode away from her driveway,
I turned and looked back.

Her future seemed, just like
her clothing, very, very black.

My motorbike - When I left Chiang Mai, I gave the motorbike to a Hmong man who had married a Lisu woman. They lived at the foreigner cemetery on the outskirts of town. He was the caretaker.

I knew him through his daughter. She sold handicrafts in the Night Market and we had had a short relationship. He also had two preteen sons. They were a nice family and were living on very limited funds.

He was shocked and more than happy when I gave him the motorbike. I got the impression, it was the nicest gift he had ever been given. He asked me, wide eyed, a half dozen times, "You are really giving it to me?" "You mean, I don't have to pay any money?" "You really mean that?"

The next day, I headed to the baan,
Following my old routine.

There, too, upon arrival,
I encountered a disturbing scene.

Several months before,
Gerald and Na had both died of AIDS.

When dopers share needles,
They pay a price for these trades.

Also, where there was one corral,
Now stood two.

When I asked about this,
I learned something new.

It has been more than twenty years since I gave up my home in Chiang Mai and returned to Germany and the USA.

I went back to Chiang Mai a half dozen times during the first ten years. The last two times I brought my future wife with me. I wanted her to know something of my past and to see the sights of Thailand.

My three Thai lady friends:

First: My Loyal Friend – She told me she had met an American through an Internet dating website. Their conversations were getting serious and he was coming to Chiang Mai to see her and meet her family.

Since then, their relationship progressed. They married and settled in Oklahoma. Recently, I understand, they retired and moved back to her hometown in Thailand. We are now Facebook friends.

A 12-year-old Lahu girl and her brother
were out one day.

They ran into a Yank
From the Druggie Lodge down the way.

The Yank said, "Your sister looks cute.
Real, real fine.

How much do I have to pay
To make your sister mine?"

He said he'd pay top dollar,
Double the normal best.

The kid said, "US $4,000."
The Yank said, "Hell, yes!"

Second: The Dress Maker – I lost track of her. On a visit, a few years after I left Chiang Mai, I found her shop had changed hands. The new owner told me, my friend had had a family emergency. Her mother became quite ill; so, she sold her shop and moved back to her home village. The new owner told me my friend had not left a forwarding address.

Third: The Government Official – She transferred back to Bangkok around the time I left for Germany.

A year later, we did meet again, in Bangkok. It was the first time we met in Bangkok and the last time we ever met. We had a warm and pleasant dinner at an upscale Thai restaurant. At the end of the meal, we sipped brandy. Our hands reached across the table and our fingers touched. We looked into each other's eyes and said, "Goodbye."

The brother hurried home,
"Gotta talk with Dad."

The father mused, "Wow.
This offer ain't bad.

Why wait two years
And only get half that sum,

Best to maximize my income.
I ain't so dumb."

The whole village got involved
Before the deal went through.

Some voiced indignation.
Others said, "It's too good to be true."

Sawadeekap
My Baan

Sawadeekap – Thai for Goodbye.

Finally, Dad got four G's and the Yank
Got sex with a twelve-year-old bride.

This split the baan. A second corral
Was built. One for each side.

My last stop, Na's family hut, before
Putting my motorbike in gear.

I bid her parents farewell,
And better fortune in the coming year.

Gerald's fair-haired hapa daughter
Had truly beautiful eyes.

Bangkok brothel procurers
Would see her as an exquisite prize.

Four G's – US $4,000.

Hapa – A mixed race person. The term is commonly used in Hawaii. Often Hapa people are quite attractive because they tend to get the best genes of both races.

The Red Lahu Girl – After I had been back in the USA for a year, I received a letter from the Red Lahu Girl. She was very depressed. She was now in her mid- twenties. She felt life was passing her by. She was sad and lonely. She wanted to know if I could find an American who would be willing to marry her. She said she just didn't fit into Thai society. With a college degree, she knew she could never live in a Lahu baan again. She felt hopeless and lonely. I wrote her a short letter saying all my friends were married and I could not offer her any suggestions. I wished her good fortune. I don't know if she ever received my letter.

I rode up a small hill,
And took a final look around.

Then, I hit the gas;
My bike was Chiang Mai bound.

From there it was CNX to BKK.
Then, back to the USA.

I sort of knew in my heart,
I'd never be back again this way.

As for Ahka Jim,
I never picked up his trail.

Hopefully, he's in a Naxi girl's arms
And not a Burmese jail.

CNX

BKK

DFW

MUN

CAN

HNL

What did my Triangle days teach me?
Really, I'm not too sure.

But, I'll gladly share more stories,
if you're paying for the beer.

Today's Triangle? Nothing's changed;
Still a playground of the drug trade.

Through it, many top police
And army get very well paid.

As for the Yards, our Green Berets
Will always hold them high;

But, long ago, our US Government
Left them out to dry.

Will I ever return to Chiang Mai? Probably not. Maybe for a visit. It was an interesting part of my life, but it was time to move on.

After leaving Thailand, I bounced in and out of Munich and the US mainland a few times. Then, as I had lived in San Antonio for a couple years before moving to Germany, and still carried a Texas driver's license and voted in Texas, I moved back to Texas. This time, to Waco, to obtain an MBA at Baylor University. Upon graduation, I was offered two positions. One offer was from a bank dealing with oil money in Almaty, Kazakhstan.

And, warlord Khun Sa?
The USA never got him, though it tried.

He shoveled enough money To the Junta
to protect his ugly hide.

Through the 1990's, he lived
In a Grand Poobah mode.

Though gradually his life of indulgent
luxury caused his power to erode.

His golf and teenage harem took on
More importance as he got older.

Gradually Khun Sa's empire was cut up
As his enemies grew bolder.

The other job offer was from China's Guangdong Province Government. The provincial government asked me to come to Guangzhou, the main trade city in South China to teach International Marketing to Chinese college students. That was in 1997. I knew China was the future, so I passed up the oil money.

The factories of Guangzhou and the adjacent Pearl River Delta produce a very large percentage of China's export consumer goods. Guangzhou's Canton Fair remains the top export fair in China.

Seeing how China has grown in the last twenty years, it seems my students learned well and now earn well. And, in retrospect, I like to think, I was a damn good teacher.

Finally, at 73, he died of middle class ills
in the Fall of 2007.

I don't know where he rots today,
But, I'll bet ten to one,

It ain't heaven.

Sawadeekap

ABOUT THE AUTHOR

Dennis M Keating has enjoyed a peripatetic lifestyle. His international perspective and eclectic enthusiasm for life come from his forty some years in Germany; Thailand; China and Hawaii.

For the last ten years, Keating and his wife, Sandy, have been living a quiet life in Waikiki. Normally, he can be found pounding his iMac keyboard, hiking the Diamond Head trail, or strolling with his wife at sunset along the sands of Waikiki.

Keating write on a diverse range of topics. His books draw upon his multifarious interests and personal experiences. Most of his books are nonfiction.

Keating's Facebook page:
https://www.facebook.com/TheHonoluluGuy/
He is happy to Friend you on Facebook.

In 2016, Keating released - *The Olympics: An Unauthorized Unsanctioned History*

In 2017, Keating released
Poetry for Men - Action Adventure Murder is a compilation of Keating's five poetry books.

Charlie Whitman was a Friend of Mine. The story of the Texas Tower Killer.

Ena Road. Murder and racism in Hawaii.

The Fulda Gap. A Cold War confrontation.

A Chicago Tale. A triple murder story.

Black Lahu. Opium, life and death in the Golden Triangle.

His email is **lostpuka@gmail.com**
His websites are:
GoldenSphere.com & **HonoluluGuy.com**

Keating owns all rights to the material in this book. For film rights, or for other reasons, please contact him.

C'est Fini, Aloha!

www.ingramcontent.com/pod-product-compliance
Lightning Source LLC
Chambersburg PA
CBHW072104270326
41931CB00010B/1454